Cultural Encounters in Translation from Arabic

TOPICS IN TRANSLATION
Series Editors: Susan Bassnett, *University of Warwick, UK*
Edwin Gentzler, *University of Massachusetts, Amherst, USA*
Editor for Translation in the Commercial Environment:
Geoffrey Samuelsson-Brown, University of Surrey, UK

Other Books in the Series
Words, Words, Words. The Translator and the Language Learner
 Gunilla Anderman and Margaret Rogers
Translation, Power, Subversion
 Román Alvarez and M. Carmen-Africa Vidal (eds)
Linguistic Auditing
 Nigel Reeves and Colin Wright
Culture Bumps: An Empirical Approach to the Translation of Allusions
 Ritva Leppihalme
Constructing Cultures: Essays on Literary Translation
 Susan Bassnett and André Lefevere
The Pragmatics of Translation
 Leo Hickey (ed.)
Practical Guide for Translators (3rd edition)
 Geoffrey Samuelsson-Brown
Written in the Language of the Scottish Nation
 John Corbett
'Behind Inverted Commas' Translation and Anglo-German Cultural Relations in the
Nineteenth Century
 Susanne Stark
The Rewriting of Njßls Saga: Translation, Ideology, and Icelandic Sagas
 Jón Karl Helgason
Time Sharing on Stage: Drama Translation in Theatre and Society
 Sirkku Aaltonen
Translation and Nation: A Cultural Politics of Englishness
 Roger Ellis and Liz Oakley-Brown (eds)
The Interpreter's Resource
 Mary Phelan
Annotated Texts for Translation: English–German
 Christina Schäffner with Uwe Wiesemann
Contemporary Translation Theories (2nd Edition)
 Edwin Gentzler
Literary Translation: A Practical Guide
 Clifford E. Landers
Translation-mediated Communication in a Digital World
 Minako O'Hagan and David Ashworth
Frae Ither Tongues: Essays on Modern Translations into Scotts
 Bill Findlay (ed.)
Practical Guide for Translators (4th edition)
 Geoffrey Samuelsson-Brown

For more details of these or any other of our publications, please contact:
Multilingual Matters, Frankfurt Lodge, Clevedon Hall,
Victoria Road, Clevedon, BS21 7HH, England
http://www.multilingual-matters.com

TOPICS IN TRANSLATION 26
Series Editors: Susan Bassnett, *University of Warwick* and
Edwin Gentzler, *University of Massachusetts, Amherst*

Cultural Encounters in Translation from Arabic

Edited by
Said Faiq

MULTILINGUAL MATTERS LTD
Clevedon • Buffalo • Toronto

For Payman, Elyas and Lanya

Library
University of Texas
at San Antonio

Library of Congress Cataloging in Publication Data
Cultural Encounters in Translation from Arabic/Edited by Said Faiq, 1st ed.
Topics in Translation: 26
Includes bibliographical references and index.
1. Arabic language–Translating. 2. Translating and interpreting. I. Faiq, Said.
II. Series.
PJ6170.C85 2004   2004002820

British Library Cataloguing in Publication Data
A catalogue entry for this book is available from the British Library.

ISBN 1-85359-744-9 (hbk)
ISBN 1-85359-743-0 (pbk)

Multilingual Matters Ltd
UK: Frankfurt Lodge, Clevedon Hall, Victoria Road, Clevedon BS21 7HH.
USA: UTP, 2250 Military Road, Tonawanda, NY 14150, USA.
Canada: UTP, 5201 Dufferin Street, North York, Ontario M3H 5T8, Canada.

Typeset by Archetype-IT Ltd (http://www.archetype-it.com).
Printed and bound in Great Britain by the Cromwell Press Ltd.

Contents

Preface

Given the long history of conflicts and misunderstanding between the West and the Arab/Islamic world, neat dichotomies developed within cultural and translation studies in the West do not seem to apply to the complex network of relations that exists between the two worlds. Both have at their disposal systems of representation laden with stereotypes of each other, with the West having had the upper hand in diffusing its representation of the Arab and Muslim Other because of the political, economic and cultural power it has enjoyed particularly since the nineteenth century and the days of direct colonial relations. In all this, translation from Arabic into Western languages has achieved very little in 'improving' cultural relations. It has largely remained influenced by negative stereotypes of the Arabs and Islam.

The chapters in this volume share the view that manipulation and deformation are common practices in translating from Arabic. Each in its own fashion, the chapters provide assessment of theories and examples of translation which demonstrate that the discourse of translating from Arabic into Western languages reflects a past and a lexicon dominated by 'fixed' perceptions of Arab culture as dead and ceased to contribute to global culture, except for terrorism, tribalism and political mischief.

The opening chapter by Said Faiq presents a rather gloomy picture of Arab–West cultural relations. The chapter reflects the historical-cum-current cultural confrontation between the two worlds (the war between the USA and its allies and Iraq is only the recent example of such a confrontation). The main conclusion of this scene and tone-setting chapter is that translation from Arabic into mainstream Western languages has proceeded according to an established system of *topoi* that has characterised both micro and macro dimensions of translation.

Chapter 2 by Richard van Leeuwen, argues that the rigidity of frameworks based entirely on orientalism have reduced the chances for cultural détente and rapprochement between the Arab world and the West. Instead, van Leewen posits the adoption of flexible theories (Bakhtin's concepts of discourse analysis and Bourdiou's literary field) that can provide useful analytical and methodological tools for the theory and practice of translation from Arabic, away from the confrontational nature of orientalism.

Chapter 3 by Ovidi Carbonell takes van Leeuwen's argument further by suggesting that concepts based on cultural studies, such as domestication and foreignisation, are not fine-tuned enough and that linguistic and text theories are not broad enough to provide the necessary apparatus for the assessment of translation from Arabic with all its discursive and ideological dimensions. Carbonell concludes that a bit of exoticism in translating from Arabic may be necessary to further strengthen the presence of Arabic literature in Western arenas besides academic/orientalist circles.

An example of Western efforts to multiply the volume of translation from Arabic into European languages is presented by Tetz Rooke in Chapter 4. The project, *Mémoires de la Méditerranée*, encourages simultaneous translations of the same Arabic text, mainly autobiographical works, into many European languages. But even here, Rooke suggests that Arab writers are still perceived as unequal to their Western counterparts: they are considered eternal beginners.

The next two chapters discuss the use of translation from Arabic for the purposes of identity formation and/or deformation. In Chapter 5, Hannah Amit-Kochavi argues that perhaps translation looks to be one of the main viable means of cultural rapprochement between the Jews and the Arabs. Two cultures, which coexisted harmoniously during the time of the Prophet Mohammad and in Muslim Spain, have known only wars and destruction for over half a century. Drawing on a number of uses of translation from Arabic into Hebrew (pseudo-translation, translation to maintain lost identities), Amit-Kochavi argues that translation from Arabic has been instrumental in forming modern Israeli/Jewish identity and thereby creating negative images of the Arab Other in Palestine. Still, Amit-Kochavi suggests that translation can reduce antagonism and create a favourable environment for peace and coexistence!

Within the context of politics and ideology of translation, Chapter 6, by Mike Holt, explores a sensitive issue in contemporary relations between the Arab/Islamic world and the West: Islamism and Islamist discourse. Holt considers the translation into English of a reference text for Islamist discourse, a translation that appears to have been carried out by Muslims and not mainstream orientalists-cum-experts on the region and its religion. In such cases, Holt points to the inherent obstacles in the mutual cultural and ideological antagonism that exists between Islamism and the West. The translation case Holt discusses shows how adherents of Islamist discourse can, to Lawrence Venuti's delight, rupture the target language (English).

The next three chapters demonstrate that even in purely linguistic and stylistic terms, translation tends to alter the Arabness of texts. In Chapter 7, Ibrahim Muhawi explores the possibility of translating Arabic folktales by interpreting style as narrative rhythm, and therefore the most natural element of oral performance for reproducing an echo of the original in the out-loud readability of the target (written) text. Muhawi considers folktale translatability as arising from the cross-pollination between the print medium and the art of folktale narration.

Chapter 8, by Hussein Abdul-Raof, discusses the untranslatability of the Qur'an, Islam's holy book. Abdul-Raof assesses a number of English translations of many Qur'anic samples in terms of the lexical, syntactic, semantic and rhetorical voids they cause in translation into English. An English Qur'an, Abdul-Raof concludes, is a translation impossibility.

Along a similar line of argument, Solomon Sara, in Chapter 9, shows that if one were to accept that literature can be manipulated through translation, the translation of linguistic terminology would, to all appearances, escape such a fate. Sara, however, demonstrates that even this area of translation from Arabic has not escaped manipulation, familiarisation and hegemony. Through the analysis of standard translations of Arabic linguistic terms, Sara concludes that the creativity and originality of native Arab linguists disappear through the use of standard Western linguistic terminology.

The final chapter, by Richard Jacquemond, ably translated from French by Philip Tomlinson, looks into the intrinsic relationship between the economy and poetics of translation between Arabic and French. Drawing on ideas from Bourdieu, Jacquemond's argument rests on the fact that the representation of Arab culture is primarily mediated and mediatised by orientalism and that translation has, therefore, oscillated between exoticisation and naturalisation.

As to acknowledgements, this modest volume involved many people and pushed the patience of some to the limit. To Susan Bassnett, my deepest thanks and gratitude for her encouragement and patience. My thanks also go to Edwin Gentzler, the Multilingual Matters Topics in Translation series editor with Susan Bassnett. Special thanks go to Maureen Tustin and Janet Bailey, from Susan Bassnett's office at Warwick University.

My thanks and gratitude naturally go to the contributors and also to Marjoka Grover and Tommi Grover, Multilingual Matters, for their support, patience and understanding. My thanks also go to Geoff Harris, Basil Hatim and Yasir Suleiman for their enthusiasm and support for the project. I am grateful to the British Academy and the League of Arab States

(London Office) for funding a seminar on the problematics of Arabic translation which inspired this volume.

Finally, I am grateful to my wife, Payman, for her unconditional and continuous support, something I have often missed to acknowledge, and to our children, Elyas and Lanya, who have completely and happily changed my life.

Said Faiq

Notes on Contributors

Hussein Abdul-Raof is a Senior Lecturer in Arabic and Qur'anic studies in the department of Arabic and Middle Eastern Studies, university of Leeds, UK. He also taught in Baghdad University (Iraq) and Salford University (UK). His research interests fall within translation theory and Arabic-English theoretical linguistics, particularly Qur'anic linguistics and stylistics. He has been a professional translator/interpreter since 1975, and has taught translation since 1980. He has published a number of books: *Subject, Theme and Agent in Modern Standard* Arabic (1998), *Qur'an Translation: Discourse, Texture and Exegesis* (2001), *Arabic Stylistics* (2001), and several articles. (h.abdul-raof@leeds.ac.uk)

Hannah Amit-Kochavi teaches classical and modern Arabic literature at Beit Berl College, Israel. Her research interests focus on translation history and intercultural contact through translation (Arabic-Hebrew) and Arabic teaching to Hebrew speakers in Israel. She has translated numerous literary works, documents and articles (Arabic-Hebrew/English) and published articles and chapters in books, most recent being: 'Hebrew translations of Palestinian literature – from total denial to partial recognition', (*TTR* XIII, 1, 2000), 'Introducing register competence into teaching Arabic as a foreign language in Israeli Hebrew speaking schools' (M. Piamenta Festschrift (ed.) 2001). (amitkoch@netvision.net.il)

Ovidi Carbonell i Cortés teaches English and Translation Studies at the University of Salamanca, Spain. His research interests focus on postcolonial translation, cultural translation, semiotics, pragmatics and sociolinguistics applied to English and Arabic translation into Spanish and Catalan. He has published *Traducir al Otro* (1997) as well as many articles and chapters in books. (ovidi@gugu.usal.es)

Said Faiq is Associate Professor of (Arabic) translation studies and Chair of the Department of English and Translation Studies at the American University of Sharjah (on leave from his lecturing post at Salford University, UK). He is Programme Director for Translation and Interpreting. He has taught in Africa, the Middle East and the UK. He has published extensively on intercultural translation and Arabic translation studies. (sfaiq@ausharjah.edu) or (s.faiq@salford.ac.uk)

Mike Holt is Head of Arabic and Lecturer in the School of Languages, Salford University (UK). He teaches Arabic, translation and Middle Eastern politics. He has published work in Arabic sociolinguistics, the language conflict in Algeria, and on language and identity in the Middle East. He is the co-editor (with Paul Gubbins) of *Beyond Boundaries: Language and Identity in Contemporary Europe* (2002). (m.j.holt@salford.ac.uk)

Richard Jacquemond teaches modern Arabic language and literature at the University of Provence (Aix-en-Provence, France). He has lived almost 15 years in Cairo as a student, head of the Translation Department of the French Cultural Bureau in Egypt, and finally Associate Researcher at the CEDEJ (Centre d'Etudes et de Documentation Economique et Juridiques). His research interests focus on modern Arabic literature, sociology of contemporary Egyptian culture and translation studies. He has published over ten translations (Arabic / French) of contemporary Egyptian and Arab writers (most recently: Sonallah Ibrahim, *Charaf ou l'Honneur* (1999), Mohammed Berrada, *Comme un été qui ne reviendra plus* (2001), Sonallah Ibrahim, *Warda* (2002), and many articles and chapters in books. (richard.jacquemond@voila.fr)

Richard van Leeuwen (Amsterdam) is a Researcher in Middle Eastern history and Arabic literature and a literary translator. His publications include: *Notables and Clergy in Mount Lebanon (1736–1840)* (1994), *Waqf and Urban Structure: The Case of Ottoman Damascus* (1999), and many articles and book chapters on history and literature. He has translated many modern Arabic novels and the *Thousand and One Nights* into Dutch. He is currently working on a research-project on the *Thousand and One Nights*. (leeuwen.poppinga@wxs.nl)

Ibrahim Muhawi teaches Arabic folklore and translation studies at the University of California, Berkeley. He has also taught in Canada, Jordan, Palestine, Tunisia and Scotland. His research interests focus on translation, Palestinian Arabic folklore and literature, and the rhetoric of oral discourse. He has published *Speak, Bird, Speak Again: Palestinian Arab Folktales* (1989 [with Sharif Kanaana]), many articles and chapters in books, including 'The metalinguistic joke: sociolinguistic dimensions of an Arabic folk genre' (1994), 'Between translation and the canon: the Arabic folktale as transcultural signifier' (2000), translated with an introduction *Memory for Forgetfulness* by Mahmoud Darwish (1995), and edited, with Yasir Suleiman, *Literature and the Nation in the Middle East*, Edinburgh: Edinburgy

University Press (forthcoming). (imuhawi@socrates.berkeley.edu or ibrahim.muhawi@ed.ac.uk)

Tetz Rooke teaches Arabic language and literature at Uppsala University in Sweden. His research interests focus on modern Arabic literature, especially on autobiographical writing. He is an award winning literary translator of Arabic novels into Swedish. *In My Childhood: A Study of Arabic Autobiography* (1997) was his published doctoral dissertation. He has also published a number of articles in books: 'Writing the boundary: Khitat al-Sham by Muhammad Kurd Ali' (2000), 'The influence of Adab on the Muslim intellectuals of the Nahda as reflected in the memoirs of Muhammad Kurd Ali (1876–1953)' (2000). (tetz.rooke@afro.uu.se) or (tetz.rooke@ebox.tninet.se)

Solomon I. Sara teaches in the Department of Linguistics, at Georgetown University, Washington, DC (USA). He has also taught at Baghdad College (Iraq). His research interests currently focus on the works of early Arab linguists: al-Khaliil and Siibawaih. He has published: *A Dictionary of Spanish, Embera, English* (2001), *A Dictionary of Phonetics: Articulatory, Acoustic Auditory: English-Arabic* (1999), *I Was A Point I Was A Circle: Book of Poetry by Houda Naamani. Preface and translation* (1993), *A Description of Modern Chaldean* (1974), *Modern Standard Arabic: Basic Course*, 19 vols (1971), and dozens of articles and chapters in books. (saras@georgetown.edu)

Philip Tomlinson is Professor of French and Head of the School of Languages, University of Salford (UK). His research interests lie mainly in early seventeenth-century French theatre, particularly the dramatist Jean Mairet, on whom he has published extensively. He has also conducted a number of language teaching research projects and has taught translation for professional purposes throughout his career. (p.tomlinson@salford.ac.uk)

Chapter 1

The Cultural Encounter in Translating from Arabic

SAID FAIQ

Introduction

The word misunderstanding, writes Rabassa (1996), is crucial in most spheres of life. Misunderstandings are said to derive from incompatibilities in processing of media which carry them: languages. Yet misunderstandings are not only the products of linguistic incompatibilities *per se* but of cultural ones as well. This means that misunderstandings generally occur in particular social structures, particular histories, and prevailing norms of language production and reception. All these can be said to make up the ingredients of the culture and the ideology subsumed within it. Culture involves the totality of attitudes towards the world, towards events, other cultures and peoples and the manner in which the attitudes are mediated. In other words, culture refers to beliefs and value systems tacitly assumed to be collectively shared by particular social groups and to the positions taken by producers and receivers of texts, including translations, during the mediation process.

Intercultural contacts that resulted in the great cultural shifts from one civilisation to another have been made possible through translation: this has meant a good deal of exchange, naturally through language. But while languages are generally prone to change over time – phonologically, morphologically, syntactically and semantically – cultures do not change fast. Cultures remain by and large prisoners of their respective pasts. Edward Said (1993: 1) succinctly argues:

> Appeals to the past are among the commonest of strategies in interpretations of the present. What animates such appeals is not only disagreement about what happened in the past and what the past was, but uncertainty about whether the past really is past, over and concluded, or whether it continues, albeit in different forms, perhaps.

This problem animates all sorts of discussions – about influence, about blame and judgement, about present actualities and future priorities.

It is in these pasts that cultures normally reside and, even if the colours, shapes and formulations of these residences change, the spirit changes little or not at all. When cultures cross and mingle through translation, these pasts come face to face and a struggle for power and influence becomes inevitable. Old formulations and modes of mediation appear on the surface, and their realisation is made possible by language.

Culture and Translation

The conception of the intrinsic relationship between language and culture in translation studies has led to theories and arguments calling for the treatment of translation as a primarily cultural act:

> That it is possible to translate one language into another at all attests to the universalities in culture, to common vicissitudes of human life, and to the like capabilities of men throughout the earth, as well as the inherent nature of language and the character of the communication process itself: and a cynic might add, to the arrogance of the translator. (Casagrande, 1954: 338)

Casagrande's statement is appropriate in putting culture at the heart of translation, but it generously overgeneralises the universality of culture being common to all men. The Lexicographer of all lexicographers decided this would not be the case: all men are therefore divided into groups each of which has its own culture and by extension its own way of perceiving and doing translation.

Taking culture and ideology as their starting point, a number of theorists have argued that the act of translating involves manipulation, subversion, appropriation and violence. Venuti (1995, 1996 and 1998), for example, argues that the very purpose and activity of translation represents violence. Postulating the concepts of domestication and foreignisation, Venuti argues that the Anglo-American translation tradition, in particular, over the last three centuries or so, has had a normalising and naturalising effect. Such an effect, Venuti stipulates, has deprived source text producers of their voice and has re-expressed foreign cultural values in terms of what is familiar, i.e. unchallenging to Western dominant culture:

> The violence of translation resides in its very purpose and activity: the reconstruction of the foreign text in accordance with values, beliefs, and representations that pre-exist in the target language, always configured in hierarchies of dominance and marginality, always

determining the production, circulation, and reception of texts. . . . Whatever difference the translation conveys is now imprinted by the target-language culture, assimilated to its positions of intelligibility, its canons and taboos, its codes and ideologies. The aim of translation is to bring back a cultural other as the same, the recognizable, even the familiar; and this aim always risks a wholesale domestication of the foreign text, often in highly self-conscious projects, where translation serves an imperialist appropriation of foreign cultures for domestic agendas, cultural, economic, political. (Venuti, 1996: 196)

Debates about translation become volatile, charged and sensitive when the notions of culture and ideology – which are always there – are marked and discussed. These two notions remain open to many assessments, one of which is the radical relativism between languages and their respective cultures. But since translation is one of the oldest occupations and/or practices, there is no escape from cultural loads that represent certain ethnic, linguistic and political groups which cross, violently or otherwise, into other ethnic, linguistic and political groups. Culture has been considered from different angles: colonial, post-colonial, modernist, postmodernist, feminist, post-feminist, orientalist, post-orientalist, and other dichotomies of X and post-X.

In post-colonial contexts, translation assumes a particularly added significance: choice of texts for translation, the use of particular discursive strategies, circulation of the translations, etc. In this respect Venuti (1994: 201–2) writes that translation is:

an inevitable domestication, wherein the foreign text is inscribed with linguistic and cultural values that are intelligible to specific domestic constituencies. This process of inscription operates at every stage in the production, circulation, and reception of the translation. It is initiated by the very choice of a foreign text to translate, always an exclusion of other foreign texts and literatures, which answers to particular domestic interests. It continues most forcefully in the development of a translation strategy that rewrites the foreign text in domestic dialects and discourses, always a choice of certain domestic values to the exclusion of others. . . . Translation is instrumental in shaping domestic attitudes towards foreign countries, attaching esteem or stigma to specific ethnicities, races, and nationalities, able to foster respect for cultural difference or hatred based on ethnocentrism, racism, or patriotism. In the long run, translation figures in geopolitical relations by establishing the cultural grounds of diplomacy, reinforcing alliances, antagonisms, and hegemonies between nations.

The Cultural Dimension in Translating from Arabic

Starting from the premise that cultural and translation studies deal with the conditions of knowledge production in one culture, and the way this knowledge is interpreted and relocated according to knowledge production in another culture, Carbonell (1996) laments the situation of translating Arabic works into mainstream European languages.

Manipulation through translation not only violates the Arabic original but also leads to the influencing of the target readers and their views of the source culture and its people. This manipulation ultimately leads to subversion of texts through translation and / or other discourses at all levels (cf. for example Jaquemond; Carbonell; Abdul-Raof; Sara, in this volume). Carbonell (1996) reports that in his comments on Burton's translation of the *Arabian Nights*, Farwell (1963/1990: 366; quoted in Carbonell, 1996), for example, says:

> The great charm of Burton's translation, viewed as literature, lies in the veil of romance and exoticism he cast over the entire work. He tried hard to retain the flavour of oriental quaintness and naivete of the medieval Arab by writing 'as the Arab would have written in English'.

Such views of translation, and by extension of readers, lead to translations that imply the production of what Carbonell calls 'subverted texts' at all levels. Translators blatantly flout all norms and maxims of shared information: they become dictators, so to speak, by altering what a group of readers is allowed to know and read, thus censoring and, to a large extent, alienating the target readers.

Reporting on personal experience of translating contemporary Arabic literature into English, Peter Clark (1997: 109) writes:

> I wanted . . . to translate a volume of contemporary Syrian literature. I . . . thought the work of 'Abd al-Salam al-'Ujaili was very good and well worth putting into English. 'Ujaili is a doctor in his seventies who has written poetry, criticism, novels and short stories. In particular his short stories are outstanding. Many are located in the Euphrates valley and depict the tensions of individuals coping with politicisation and the omnipotent state. . . . I proposed to my British publisher a volume of 'Ujaili's short stories. The editor said, 'There are three things wrong with the idea. He's male. He's old and he writes short stories. Can you find a young female novelist?' Well, I looked into women's literature and did translate a novel by a woman writer even though she was and is in her eighties.

The assumed and imaginary basis in most representations of all that is

Arab and Islamic lies in the Western obsession with fixed texts and its fixation with the mechanisms of this fixedness, which all non-Western cultures are said to lack. Translating Arabic texts, with specific traditions for production, reception and circulation, into fixed texts has meant taking liberties, being invisible, violent, appropriationist and subverter to shift the texts into mainstream world culture and literature. World culture and literature means, of course, the Western canons of production that also stand as signs of universalism and humanism (cf. Asad, 1995).

When Arab writers, like the superb critic of the Middle Eastern oil based societies Munif, are translated into English, critics either ignore or denigrate their writings. Dallal (1998) quotes a John Updike remark about Munif's outstanding *Cities of Salt*: 'It is unfortunate . . . that Mr Munif . . . appears to be . . . insufficiently Westernized to produce a narrative that feels much like what we call a novel.' Such an attitude stems from the one-sided, still current stereotypical ideology based on universalism, unitarism, and the homogeneity of human nature. This ideology marginalises and excludes the distinctive and unique characteristics of Arab societies and their discursive traditions. What Updike is saying is that the West needs to satisfy itself that it knows its natives: it is others who should adapt to its norms in order to be welcomed as members of universalism and world culture and literature. The Western centric assumptions about others – races, nationalities, literatures – has provided the site for critiques of representations, language and ideological control towards writers from places like the Arab world. These assumptions return time and again to haunt the production, reception and circulation of Arabic texts, and in turn complicate the issue of translation (cf. Jacquemond, 1992).

Though the West has, in the 1980s and 1990s, opened up to Third World peoples, cultures and texts – Latinos, for example – the literatures of the Arab-Islamic world remain generally marginalised, despite the enormous and persistent attention – almost hysteria – accorded to Arabs and to Islam. Translation from Arabic still proceeds along familiar and established scripts whereby:

> stereotyping, strategies of signification and power: the network in which a culture is fashioned does appear as a texture of signs linked by endless connotations and denotations, a meaning system of inextricable complexity that is reflected, developed and recorded in the multifarious act of writing. (Carbonnel, 1996: 81)

In his translation of Naguib Mahfouz's novel *yawma qutila z-za'iim* (The Day the Leader was Killed/Assassinated), André Miquel explains in his foreword to the French-language reader that he kept footnotes to the very minimum. Yet Jacquemond (1992) counted 54 footnotes in a 77-page translation. What transpires is that the translator-cum-orientalist expert assumes total ignorance on the part of his reading constituencies, and proceeds to guide them through assumed authoritative knowledge of an unfathomable world where backwardness and the assassination of peacemakers are the norms. But this would be acceptable compared with Edward Fitzgerald's 'infamous comment' on the liberties he had allowed himself to take with his version of *The Rubaiyat of Omar Khayam*, 'really [they] need a little art to shape them' (Bassnett, 1998a: 78).

This is most clear in the assessment of the Arab/Muslim character by the Victorian Orientalist Richard Burton, who provided the images he grew up with before he ever met an Arab or Muslim person:

> Our Arab at his worst is a mere barbarian who has not forgotten the savage. He is a model mixture of childishness and astuteness, of simplicity and cunning, concealing levity of mind under solemnity of aspect. His stolid instinctive conservatism grovels before the tyrant rule of routine, despite the turbulent and licentious independence which ever suggests revolt against the ruler; his mental torpidity, founded upon physical indolence, renders immediate action and all manner of exertion distasteful; his conscious weakness shows itself in an overweening arrogance and intolerance. His crass and self-satisfied ignorance makes him glorify the most ignoble superstitions, while acts of revolting savagery are the natural results of a malignant fanaticism and a furious hatred of every creed beyond the pale of Al-Islam. (quoted in Karim, 1997: 159)

It is barely conceivable that a person like the informed, know-all Burton, bothered to translate from the language of a people with such characteristics. Moreover, it is inconceivable not to link Burton's assessment with the social fabric of Britain and Europe at that time. After all, the inquisition in Spain targeted mainly Muslims who, for centuries, tolerated and protected non-Muslims. Burton's and Fitzgerald's assessments are instances of how the Other Arab and Islam are perceived, and how their culture is systematically represented in ready-made scripts prevalent in the Western culture at all levels: education, poetics and politics. In this respect, Niranjana (1992: 71) fittingly writes:

> The naturalising, dehistoricising move is, of course, accompanied by a situating of the 'primitive' or the 'Oriental' in a teleological scheme that shows them to be imperfect realisations of the Spirit or of Being.

This is exactly what Christian polemics have been propounding about Islam, its Prophet, Muhammad, and by extension Arabs: attributing violence, salaciousness, and irrationality to them. Bhabha (1994: 82) aptly

argues that: 'It is recognizably true that the chain of stereotypical signification is curiously mixed and split, polymorphous and perverse, an
articulation of multiple belief.' Recall Burton's assessment and Clark's
experience!

An example of how translation deformed an Arabic indigenous literary
genre is the *qaSida*, that 'canonized genre of Arabic poetry, which has never
been satsfactorily translated in the West, because it has no obvious generic
equivalent' (Lefevre, 1990: 25). The *qaSida* was forced into translation,
losing its status with the advent of free poetry because of Western influence
in the Arab world with imperialism, and the readiness of Arab élites to
embrace Western poetical genres to the detriment of the *qaSida*, a genre that
lasted since pre-Islam. Lefevere (1990: 26) again:

> Language is not the problem. Ideology and poetics are, as are cultural
> elements that are clear, or seen as completely 'misplaced' in what
> would be the target culture version of the text to be translated. One
> such element is the camel dung mentioned in Labid's *qasida*, which can
> hardly be expected to make a 'poetic' impression on Western readers.
> Carlyle, the English Victorian translator, leaves it out altogether . . .
> German translators, on the other hand, try to find a cultural analogy,
> but with little success: the solution is worse than the problem: 'German
> scholars, familiar with the peasants of their own land, where the size of
> the dung heap is some indication of the prosperity of the farmer,
> merely transported to the desert the social values of Bavaria'.

This domestication denies the *qaSida* its status as a tool for the criticism
of sociopolitical problems of society, a role not restricted to Arab culture
alone, as Bassnett (1998b: 57) writes:

> Poets have very different functions in different societies, and this is a
> factor that translators need to bear in mind. In former communist
> Eastern Europe, for example, poetry sold in big print-runs (now
> replaced by western soft-porn and blockbuster crime novels); poets
> were significant figures, who often spoke out against injustice and
> oppression.

This is precisely what Arab poets and their *qaSaa'id* (sing. *qaSida*) had
exercised in the Arab world until the modern age and the forced desire to
join world literature and its genre: the novel. Some of the explosive forms of
nationalism which the Arab world has seen show that the novel is not the
only means for modernity and nation building (cf. Dallal, 1998).

Even the award of the Nobel Prize to Naguib Mahfouz does not escape
the cultural attitude of the West towards all that is Arab. Thomas (1998:
105) sums up the feelings of many an Arab that the prize clearly

supports the view of a literature dependent on the West for its forms. In this regard it is intersting to consider Naguib Mahfoudh – the only Arab writer to have been given the full western seal of approval . . . He worked as a censor throughout the Nasser and Sadat eras, eras not noted for liberal attitudes to the arts or critical awareness.

But this prize, regardless of who thinks what, never created serious interest in contemporary Arabic literature or the turmoil, social, economic, political, etc. the Arab world is going through. Said (1995: 98) writes:

> now that the act has worn thin, Mahfouz has more or less been dropped from discussion – without having provoked even the more venture-some literari into finding out which other writers in Arabic might be worth looking into. Where, after all, did Mahfouz come from? It is impossible not to believe that one reason for this odd state of affairs is the longstanding prejudice against Arabs and Islam that remains entrenched in Western, and especially American, culture.

For centuries, Arabic has been made to conform to the prevailing system at work in the West. Interestingly the system, despite rapid changes in Western societies in terms of tolerence, multiculturalism and multi-ligualism which underpin translation from Arabic and writings in Western languages about the Arabs and Islam, has remained prisoner of the same discursive, poetical and ideological framework, reminiscent of Fitzgerald's and Burton's comments. The Arab world and Islam are still translated / represented through monolingual eyes.

Arab culture and Islam, distanced by time, space and language(s), are usually carried over – made to cross over – into a Western tradition as an originary moment and image within a master narrative of western discourse full of ready-made stereotypes and clichés (cf. Layoun, 1995; Said, 1997). This situation has persisted although the Arab world is a melting pot of nations, languages, dialects, constituencies, religions and religious practices, and ideologies; a world that has also seen most forms of appropriation and subversion, including physical violence through the many wars over centuries, not least the conflicts of the opening years of this century.

It can perhaps be argued that such attitudes of the West towards the Arab world, through translation and representation, can be rationalised on the basis that two different cultures with two separate pasts have clashed, and continue to do so. The Europeans colonised the Arab lands for decades, and the post-colonial situation is different only in terms of the fact that, after the Second World War, the United States became in many ways the guardian, or custodian, of the Arab world. Given such a premise, one can argue that manipulatory and subversive representations of one side to the other may be taken as part of the scheme of history. After all, without such clashes, manipulations and subversions history would not have moved. The problem, however, is that representations of the Arab world, and Islam, have changed very little. The same discursive strategies still prevail. The representations of Arabs and Islam by and/or for the West are not just accounts of different places, cultures and societies, but more importantly, they are projections of the West's own fears and desires masqueraded as objective knowledge: consider for instance how the words *jihad* and *fatwa* have been injected with meanings that reinforce the centuries-old clichés.

This is the argument that Venuti (1995; 1998) tries to expand and provide solutions for. Venuti's notions of domestication, the negation of the spirit of the source language and culture in the target ones, and foreignisation, the refusal of the dominant master discourse and resort to marginal linguistic and literary values at home, i.e. target language and literary values, refer to Bassnett's (1991) view that the authoritarian relationships between translators and what they deem inferior source cultures were compatible with the rise and spread of colonialism. But though colonialism, in its conventional sense at least, is no more, the authoritarian relationships still persist.

Nawal al-Saadawi, the most translated Arab writer today after Naguib Mahfouz, is another example. Her fame in the West does not stem from her status as a writer who criticises social practices, particularly women's issues, in the Arab world, but primarily from her accounts of 'clitoridectomy': accounts in demand in the West. This has led Saadawi to tailor her writings in response to the pressures and appeal of the Western marketplace (cf. Dallal, 1998).

What further complicates the cultural antagonism between Arabic (in an inclusive fashion) and the West (also in an inclusive fashion) is the disparity between the books written about the Arab-Islamic world in mainstream European languages by the self-appointed experts, as well as by the growing number of Arabs writing in accordance with the norms of the master discourses of European languages (cf. Faiq, 2000, 2001, 2003; Jacquemond, this volume), and the number of books actually translated from Arabic. The diminutive proportion of actual translations from Arabic has nonetheless to conform to the dominant Western representational ideology of all that is Arab and Islamic; a situation that has led to Arabs writing in Arabic but for translation.

Because these texts are either published in or written specifically for the West, the issue is whether the dominant culture will accept and interact equitably with them, or whether it will try to force them to assimilate to its value systems: its master discourse. Such texts have received attention from Western academic and journalistic critics, as well as the general readership, even though only a few writers maintain noticeable presence in the Western literary arena. This is because for such texts to achieve a status comparable with that achieved by Tahar Ben Jelloun's *La nuit sacrée* (winner of the 1987 prestigious Prix Goncourt), they need to conform to: (a) dominant Western representations of Arab culture and society, and (b) dominant Western ideological moral and aesthetic values. Though *La nuit sacrée* has been described by some as the model of North African literature that is both resister and liberator, it was the Prix Goncourt that located it within world literature and hastened its translation back into Arabic by and for people who undoubtedly share Ben Jelloun's tastes. Even its celebrated bilingualism or 'translingualism' does not make it oppositional to French cultural representations of the Arabs and Islam: 'Modern world culture has no difficulty in accommodating unstable signs and domesticated exotica, so long as neither conflicts radically with systems of profit' (Asad, 1995: 331).

Discussing the discursive strategies of the female Arab writer, Hanan al-Shaykh in her novel *Women of Sand and Myrrh*, Dallal (1998: 8), for example, appropriately writes:

> That *Women of Sand and Myrrh* was written specifically for English-speaking audiences is clear in the opening chapter. References specific to Western culture which would be unfamiliar to Arabs go unexplained, whereas references to customs or practices specific to Arab contexts are consistently accompanied by explanations. Suha explains why 'the [imported] soft toys and dolls had all been destroyed' by the authorities: 'every one that was meant to be a human being or animal or bird [was confiscated] since it was not permissible to produce distortions of God's creatures'. This explanation of a particular interpretation of Islam (or outright fabrication, as most Arab Muslims would believe) used by the Gulf regimes would need no explanation for Arab audiences. However, the narrators' references to 'Barbie dolls and Snoopies and Woodstocks' would not be recognized by most in the Arab world, and yet are left without explanation.

Translation from Arabic, even of pragmatic texts as defined by Lefevere (1996), still makes immediate use of the fixed structures and vocabulary that have persisted for many centuries, with the addition, during the last four decades or so, of the image Arab / Islam = fundamentalism. The Arabs and Islam are not only normally translated into established discursive strategies, and a range of allusiveness for the target language readers, but also into the very norms of choosing what to translate, ways of publishing and reviewing: recall Updike's comment on Munif. In this respect Venuti (1996: 196) draws attention to the power of translation to (re)constitute and cheapen foreign texts, to trivialise and exclude foreign cultures, and thus potentially to figure in racial discrimination and ethnic violence, international political confrontations, terrorism, war.

What Venuti lists applies to the translation and representation of the Arabs and Islam. The manipulation, most certainly intended, of simple words in Arabic (*jihad* and *fatwa*, for example) triggers the images of violence, terrorism and fundamentalism; labels among many that are pretexts but serve as pretexts reserved for the Arabs and Islam (cf. Zlateva, 1990 for a discussion of the notions of pre-text and pretext). The choice of what to translate from Arabic, even with a Nobel Prize in Literature, is still prisoner of the old/new ideology of ethnocentric domestication of a familiar yet foreign culture. Recall Peter Clark's experience!

Arabic texts chosen for translation, and those written by Arabs mainly in English or French, are normally well received in the West because they are full of nights with and images of the dead and ghosts; precisely what mainstream orientalist discourse maintains in its depiction of the Arabs and Islam.

Ghosts are the remains of the dead. They are echoes of former times and former lives: those who have died but still remain, hovering between erasure of the past and the indelibility of the present – creatures out of time. Muslims too, it seems, are often thought to be out of time: throwbacks to medieval civilizations who are caught in the grind and glow of 'our' modern culture. It is sometimes said that Muslims belong to cultures and societies that are moribund and have no vitality – no life of their own. Like ghosts they remain with us, haunting the present. (Sayyid, 1997: 1)

Conclusion

Post-colonial contexts offer good examples of the interdependence of cultural manifestations in which dominant and dominated co-exist. In this cultural traffic, foreign works are actually assumed and consumed more, and differences demarcated. Thus intercultural translation has helped in breaking down hierarchies between cultures and peoples, but at the same it has given rise and form to discourses of both domination and resistance, becoming therefore the interplay of cross-cultural pride and prejudice.

Yet, and as far as translation from Arabic is concerned, there is, it seems, a continuous interaction between Western representations of Arabic culture and the linguistic, cultural and political economy of translation from Arabic. Even the writings in French or English of Arabs tend to fit two criteria: the dominant ideology and poetics of translation from Arabic and the dominant stereotypical representations of Arab-Islamic culture. These two criteria have been framed by the numerous translations of the *One Thousand and One Nights* which, for almost two centuries, has undeniably been the main source of Western representations of Arab culture and by extension Islam, as a cultural ensemble, in both the extremely negative (violence, barbarism, etc.) and the positive, but inherently negative (exoticism and sensualism).

Perhaps an appropriate way of concluding this chapter is to cite some actual figures of the state of translating from Arabic into English and French, the two major Western languages. Venuti (1995: 14) shows the number of Arabic works translated in 1982, 1983 and 1984. In 1982, 298 Arabic works were translated in the United States out of a total of 54,198; 322 in 1983 out of a total of 55,618; and 536 in 1984 out of a total of 52,405 translated foreign works. These figures which relate to a living language and a contemporary culture look miniscule compared with translations of classical Greek and Latin works whose numbers were 839, 1116 and 1035 for the three years respectively. In France, the *One Thousand and One Nights* was translated 78 times between 1948 and 1968, compared with 14 translations of classical works, and 19 of modern Arabic works. And, in 1986, 529 out of 18,000 titles published in France related in one way or another to the Arab-Islamic world, but only 29 were translated from Arabic (cf. Jacquemond, 1992).

Not surprisingly, translation keeps reinforcing the same representations orientalism has created: it inscribes in the structure of language itself, English, French and the Arabic of those who write for translation, the images of a complicated orient, irremediably strange and different; yet familiar and exotic. At the same time, such acts of translation allow orientalism to reassert its status as the indispensable and authorised mediator between Arab/Islamic and Western cultures.

The poetics and discourse of translating from Arabic, and mainstream representation and interpretation of Arabs and Islam, lead to what Said (1997: 163) calls 'cultural antipathy':

> Today Islam is defined negatively as that with which the West is radically at odds, and this tension establishes a framework radically limiting knowledge of Islam. So long as this framework stands, Islam, as a vitally lived experience for Muslims, cannot be known.

The outcome of this cultural antipathy towards the Arabs and Islam is manifest in the minuscule translations from Arabic except, of course, for those texts that further reinforce the privileged representations that have acquired the status of facts. The discursive strategies and transparencies, in translating all that is Arab and Islamic, tend to refer to static and timeless societies and peoples, which are turned into naturalised and dehistoricised images within master Western narratives.

Is there hope for projects that would make translation a site for interaction, reassessment and reconstruction between two proud hegemonic systems, cultures, namely Arabic and Western? Probably not, as the following advert, which appeared in March 1998 in a newspaper addressed to the student population in the north-west of England, shows:

Arab NET
http://www.arab.net
A bulging omniscient resource of rare detail comprising thousands of pages on North Africa and the Middle East, their peoples, geography, economy, history, culture, *and of course, camels.* (emphasis added)

Chapter 2

The Cultural Context of Translating Arabic Literature

RICHARD VAN LEEUWEN

Introduction

It was in 1988, shortly before Naguib Mahfouz was awarded the Nobel Prize for literature, that for the first time I was confronted with the complex cultural and political implications of translating Arabic literature. During an exploratory visit to Cairo, I met various, often contradictory, attitudes towards the translation of Arabic literature into European languages, which showed that the transfer of literary texts from one culture to another is a highly politicised activity, which touches not only on historical, political and cultural relations but also on sensitive issues of cultural identification and self-representation. Moreover, literary translations and cultural exchange are tightly linked to power relations and to hierarchic divisions between hegemonic and dominated societies.

The different attitudes towards literary translation were not only connected with the problems of intercultural exchange, but also with the tensions in Egyptian society in the late 1980s. Radical Islamists had staged a fierce campaign against the supposed immorality proliferated through the arts. Theatre, singing and dancing were condemned, since they provoked frivolity, licentiousness, and promiscuity. Accusations were also directed against literature, and a large number of Arab authors were reproached for propagating a secularist world-view hostile to religion in general and to Islam in particular. There was a feeling among Islamist movements that these reprehensible activities derived from Western influences and increasing servility to Western materialistic culture. These influences, it was held, were threatening the 'true', Islamic identity of Egypt and the Arab world.

Discussions of this kind obviously affected the position of writers, who were not only attacked in the ongoing polemics but also participated in debates on the cultural orientation of the country and relations with Europe. As far as the translation of literature was concerned, some would stress the danger that European translation programmes would only be an extension of efforts at consolidating European supremacy, of imperialist schemes to dominate Egyptian culture and to endorse orientalist representations of the Arabs. European translators, it was said, were inclined to select titles that would appeal to public bias and to forget about a faithful representation of the Egyptian and by extension Arab 'soul'.

This attitude was strengthened by the idea of some authors that, in literature, Europe had ceased to provide the models. The European novel had exhausted its potential and had lost its relevance for the dilemmas facing the Arab world. Authors preferred to direct their glance at literature in Latin America and Asia, which reflected problems and issues similar to those in Arab societies, and which no longer considered Europe as setting the standards for literature. In contrast, other writers emphasised the importance of strong cultural ties with Europe and of literary translations. Many authors offered their work for translation, perhaps out of personal motives, while others saw the interest of European intellectuals in Arab culture as an important force counterbalancing the growing interference of Islamist movements in Egyptian culture. Embedding Arabic literature in international intellectual networks would protect authors from the 'enemy within', the Islamists, who propagated the moral purgation of society and culture.

How can these contradictory attitudes be explained? What is the context that gives literature and literary translation such a vital function in debates on cultural orientation? Why are authors so sensitive about questions of translation and cultural exchange? In this chapter I will attempt to analyse the conditions in which literary translation from Arabic into European languages has developed in the perspective of European-Arab relations. Special attention will be given to identity and to mutual representations of the Other. On the level of theory, the points of reference will be Edward Said (1979) and his concept of orientalist discourse, Mikhail Bakhtin (1994) and his cultural dialogism, and the idea of the literary field conceived by Pierre Bourdieu (1991, 1993, 1996).

Translation and Cultural Exchange in the *nahDa* Period

Although novelistic tendencies can be perceived in Arabic literature before the 19th century, the main achievement of Arab authors from the second half of the 19th century until the present day is the creation of a tradition of the Arabic novel. This statement implies, firstly, that the Arabic novelistic tradition is seen as a product of the *nahDa* period, the phase of cultural reform under the influence of increasing contacts between Europe and the Arab world; and, secondly, that the Arabic novel is generally speaking derived from European models and European definitions of the genre. These observations have important consequences for the evaluation of the position of Arab writers today. They are, so to speak, borne by the interaction between two cultures and by a very specific phase in the history of the Arab world characterised by European hegemony, efforts at reform and the political disintegration of the Ottoman Empire. The Arabic novel was, one can say, the result of a protracted and broad social crisis and of the awareness that the world had radically changed.

The period of the *nahDa* and especially the relations between Europe and the Arab world in the 19th century are often analysed in terms of 'orientalism', formulated by Edward Said. This approach holds that the Arab world was part of an imaginary Orient, created by the hegemonic cultural and academic discourse in Europe and subservient to European expansionist interests. From the 18th century onwards, a systematic set of representations of this Orient was developed, which transformed the Arab world into a panorama of stereotypes and which replaced interest in the true nature of Arab societies and legitimised European dominance in the Arab world. Moreover, orientalist discourse provided Europe with the concept of the Other which could be utilised to formulate a specifically European identity and a Eurocentric world-view. The representation of the Orient was the reflection of a self-image which became one of the mainstays of European cultural self-awareness.

It has been remarked that the *nahDa* period, from the first half of the 19th century onwards, was predominantly and essentially shaped by the translation movement, consisting of more or less systematic translation of European texts into Arabic. The influence of translation in many fields gave rise to a kind of schizophrenic culture, in which the intellectual élite was shaped by foreign outlooks and became estranged from the 'traditional' indigenous corpus of knowledge. As I have shown elsewhere (1981, 1998a, 2000a, 2000b), at least in some cases the European view of the Orient, with the concomitant conceptions of progress and civilisation, were adopted and internalised by Arab intellectuals, and European forms of political and economic organisation became models for reformist leaders. According to some, the importance of translated texts prevented the emergence of an authentic discourse on Arab identity, since the problem of identity was wholly seen through the prism of European conceptions. The mirror-image of the Other, as conceived by the Europeans, became more or less a reality, because the 'Orientals' themselves tried to conform to it.

This view of translation in the context of cultural hegemony stresses the importance of hierarchic relations: texts of a dominant culture were transferred to a dominated culture where they had a disproportionately large impact. Supported by the military, economic and political power of the European nations, they became the driving force of the hegemonic culture in the Arab world, dispelling the need for Europeans to revise their conceptions of the areas they ruled. Cultural exchange consisted of a one-way flow of information, knowledge and images, imposing the Eurocentric world-view on the colonial and semi-colonial areas. Cultural exchange, therefore, became a form of cultural expansionism and an extension of imperialist schemes. This vision of the role of translations in the history of European-Arab relations is still widespread among Arab intellectuals.

The framework of the orientalist discourse has its merits, but it also has important flaws. It has been remarked by many authors (cf. MacKenzie, 1995; Sprinker, 1992; Turner, 1994) that Edward Said's theoretical foundations are eclectic and not consistent. His analysis of texts leaves too little room for variations and currents diverging from the mainstream. It is in some respects contradictory: for instance, when Said argues that orientalism is fixed in the European subconsciousness, while at the same time it is manipulated to endorse certain political interests. It is also rather mechanistic, leaving little opportunity for change, since orientalism is an essential part of the European discursive structure and inseparable from the European self-image. As long as power relations remain as they are, nobody can escape Said's orientalist propensity, not even those who criticise orientalist discourse. In a way, the anti-orientalist critique strengthens and ossifies the fundamental dichotomy that was, in its own view, created and reproduced by orientalist discourse, since it is now an essential part of the European mind.

A less rigid view of intercultural relations can be founded on the theories of Mikhail Bakhtin, especially on his concepts of 'dialogism' and 'genre', which until now have only rarely been used to analyse the cultural exchange between Europe and the Arab world. According to Bakhtin, language acquires its meaning through 'dialogue', a dualistic speech act in specific contexts. The production of meaning through the dialogic process is not limited to individuals, but also occurs in groups, societies, nations and cultures, by interaction and the exchange of interpretations. Images of others are formulated by a two-sided process in which the ultimate significance is a combination of interpretations of the 'utterances' of the other. The meanings and images, which determine our view of reality are subsequently organised in genres governed by certain conventions and by the continuing process of dialogue. Genres are the structurally organised components of our view of the world and also the vehicle by which this view is reproduced and transferred from one generation to the next. They contain the representations of reality and the conceptions held in common by the members of specific groups (cf. Holquist, 1994; Morson & Caryl, 1990).

The most complex of genres, according to Bakhtin, is the novel, since it is essentially 'polyphonic', that is, it allows the interference of various voices and various interpretations in a single text, in contrast to the 'monophonic' texts of myths and epics, which represent a monolithic and stagnant view of the world. The great rupture in Western culture is marked by the transition from the epic genre to the novelistic genre in the early renaissance, when texts were no longer part of a distant, mythical past, but directly related to reality and daily life. In contrast to epics, novels are not self-sufficient wholes; they are so tightly related to the here and now that they are essentially open-ended, always referring to an unknown future. The novel is also tightly related to the search for identity and to an essential scepticism about the definitions of the self and fixed images of reality. In fact, it is this scepticism which inspired the transition from the epic to the novelistic genre, and which was in its turn engendered by the confrontation of the epic 'mind' with the Other, forcing it to discard its monophonic and monolithic outlook and incorporate other voices into it. Thus the novel is intimately linked to the travelogue, as an expression of individual experiences and representations of others *vis-à-vis* the self.

It is clear that Bakhtin's system of generic formation is much more open and flexible than Said's paradigm of orientalism. It is dynamic and less normative and it is based on interaction. In the case of European-Arab relations, it would imply that images of the Orient are not just the monopoly of the Europeans; these images were produced rather by a cultural encounter based on observation, interpretation and dialogic exchange and subsequently organised within the generic system. This system continued to develop and was repeatedly adapted to include new events, observations, texts, etc. It may be argued that the idea of genre to some extent overlaps with Said's use of discourse, and perhaps it could be defended that a form of orientalist genre arose in the age of European expansion, which reproduced the generally accepted stereotypes of the Orient. The difference would be, however, that the Bakhtinian idea of generic conventions is less static. Genres can and do dissolve into new genres, conventions change according to circumstances and the dialogic context, and divergent voices can be seen not as anomalies in the system but as contributions to a dialogue which did not become predominant.

Bakhtin's model can be useful for an analysis of the *nahDa* period in two respects. Firstly, just as the European novelistic tradition emerged from the widening of Europe's world-view in the ages of expansion, the rise of the Arabic novel can be related to the intensification of contacts between the Arab world and Europe. In the course of the 19th century, the dialogue between an expansionist Europe and the fragmenting political structures in the Middle East produced new sets of meanings, which shook the old systems of generic conventions both in Europe and in the Arab world. In Europe several waves of exoticism followed, which repeated established images of the Orient but also added new ones. In the Middle East it resulted in a period of 'occidentalism' consisting of translations, reforms according to Western models, a reinterpretation of the traditional heritage from a new perspective, and the development of new genres. Cultural exchange was especially conducive to a debate on cultural identity, which was not merely copied from European models and concepts but always took account of authenticity, tradition and forms of self-assertion. An important contribution to this discussion was provided by the main realistic and imaginary travel accounts which, as in Europe some ages before, sowed the seeds of the Arabic novelistic tradition. Thus all the constituent elements of the rise of the novelistic genre, as conceived by Bakhtin, were there. It was born naturally out of changing circumstances.

Secondly, the process of translating texts can be seen in a different perspective. Translations are not merely aimed at cultural appropriation, but are rather points of reference in a broader context of relations and a means to rethink and revise existing practices and ideas. The texts will never be understood or interpreted according to the society that produced them, but will always be placed in the receiving society and be utilised according to its specific needs. Moreover, translations are never meant to convey a full survey of another culture, but rather to provide elements, which somehow add to the images of a culture and as such provide material for self-definition. A translated text never fully assimilates into existing genres of a culture, but always contributes to the dynamism of a genre as an element functioning within the dialogic process. A text, moreover, never retains its original meaning; its interpretation changes somewhere between its intended meaning and the models to which it is related in the receiving culture. The reception of a text is therefore never predestined, but is rather one of the driving forces in producing representations of others and definitions of the self.

One of the questions that arise from this summary of Bakhtin's concept of dialogism is how it refers to power. How do hierarchic power relations affect dialogue? Is the exchange of images and texts related to political and economic power? Bakhtin himself does not go into these questions but, especially in the discussion of European-Arab relations, they seem to be of crucial importance. Obviously, lack of balance in the power relations between two societies does not lead to a stagnation of dialogue, turning exchange into a one-sided enforcement of ideas. It would seem rather that unequal power relations do not affect dialogism as a source of meaning but do affect the cultural goods that are exchanged. Orientalism in Europe and occidentalism in the Arab world are two sides of the same dialogic process, although their manifestations are different. Orientalism was usually directed at the external manifestations of Arab-Islamic culture and associated with various stereotypes of the Orient which had developed over time, such as mysticism, romantic barbarism, sensual sophistication, etc. Occidentalism was, in contrast, focused on the sciences, technology, warfare and socio-economic organisation, all associated with stereotypes of the Europeans, such as a lack of spiritual values, calculated materialism, technical and organisational ingenuity and moral laxity. It seems that the power relations between the Arab world and Europe added elements to the two existing systems of representations, but they were elements of different kinds, adapted to what the other possessed that could accommodate one's needs. Apart from the different nature of the cultural 'commodities' that were exchanged, the impact of these commodities on the receiving society also differed. Therefore, what was a temporary vogue in one culture became the essence of cultural reform in the other.

The significance of imported ideas, images and texts is thus related to power relations; but how are interpretation and categorising organised? Receptions of the images produced by dialogue should be absorbed by an internal 'market' of ideas and texts in the two societies. Power relations between societies are related to power structures in these societies which determine the trade in cultural goods and their distribution and 'value'. The processes that regulate this are aptly described by Pierre Bourdieu, whose notion of the 'field' of literary production links power to taste and the economic and symbolic valuation of cultural products. All producers of cultural goods are involved, including artists, patrons, publishers, art-dealers, critics, the public, etc. They define the standards of the arts according to economic value, fashion, and symbolic connotations. Changes are always a reflection of the dynamics of power relations. Young participants struggle to replace vested interests by new values, while the older ones try to retain their positions of authority. Furthermore, the interaction between tradition and avant-garde contributes to the continual transformation of culture (cf. Jenkins, 1992).

Perhaps the clearest way of illustrating the functioning of cultural exchange is to imagine that each society is a participant in the culture of the other. It would appear that during the 19th century Arab-Islamic culture was present in European culture(s), especially in literature, painting, architecture and academic research. To take literature as an example, every French author of repute, from Lamartine to Gautier, embraced orientalism in his work by publishing an oriental travelogue, an exotic novel, or an Eastern *diwan*. Exoticism, with its various connotations, provided the basis for the Romantic Movement and was supported by expansion of the colonial empires, new opportunities for travel and increasing imports of Eastern products. Significantly, however, orientalism did not aim to present a faithful picture of Islam or the Arab world but rather to give a highly subjective representation which would illustrate a European state of mind. Arab-Islamic culture had a decisive impact in European culture, but it had already been internalised to fulfil a specific psychological and social role.

In the Arab world, in the 19th century, European culture seemed to be the symbol of progress in both culture and politics. From the beginning the idea of progress was associated with mechanisms of power, with reform and with intensified contacts with Europe. These ambitions were supported by the European powers for whom reform prepared the way to penetrate Arab economies and politics. Military hegemony was inseparable from political interference, economic expansion and the enhancement of cultural influence. Soon a Westernised élite shaped Arab culture, absorbing as many aspects of European culture as possible, while at the same time discussing authentic cultural identities and the nature of tradition. Here, too, travellers played a crucial role, conveying images in a didactic discourse on the tensions between progress and tradition. Even when colonial malpractices against Europe evoked feelings of bitterness in many parts of the Arab world, the cultural and political debates remained governed by occidentalism, since this was linked to power (cf. Larrimendi & Parrilla, 1997).

If we compare the Arab and European cultural scenes, the first thing that is apparent is that in both cases they are prominent participants in the culture of the other, but they function in different ways. This is partly because of the cultures themselves, since in Europe there has been a strong tendency toward the emancipation of culture, that is, its dissociation from politics. In the Arab world the reverse is true: a strong connection has always existed between political dominance and cultural symbols; it was a symbiosis between authorities, intellectuals and Western culture which in a relatively short period revolutionised Arab culture. Certainly, the transformation was buttressed by a relatively small élite and hardly touched popular culture, at least in the 19th century. Thus a dichotomy was formed, which linked modern culture to state power and which prevented the rise of autonomous culture.

With regard to literature, the situation outlined above implied that in Europe the Orient was mainly a source of aesthetic or even ornamental representations, seldom giving rise to fundamental questions related to cultural identity and political issues. In the Arab world, on the contrary,

Western cultural models became the substance of literature, the basis for a new genre under the auspices of a new political hegemony.

Translation and Cultural Exchange

Analysis of the *nahDa* period gives an idea of the complexities involved in the translation of modern Arabic literature. Firstly, modern Arabic literature is associated with a relatively small élite of Westernized intellectuals in the Arab world; secondly, it is seen as vital in the debates on Arab-Islamic cultural identities, and in the dislodging of old concepts and their reinterpretation; thirdly, modern literature was never part of 'autonomous' literary production but has always been associated with political and ideological debates; fourthly, translation of literary texts is affected by the interaction of two literatures which operate differently and which tend to regulate the reception of images of the Other; fifthly, translated texts are part of a process of interpreting and determining meanings in a cultural dialogue which prevents appropriation of meanings by one of the participants; finally, all these issues are directly related to questions of cultural identity and established symbols of power.

The continuing relevance of cultural exchange was shown by the discussions accompanying the award of the Nobel Prize for literature to Naguib Mahfouz in 1988. The laureation of Egypt's foremost novelist was hailed by some who saw it as a proof of appreciation of Arabic literature in the West, which could end the Arabs' feelings of minority complex with regard to hegemonic cultural standards of Europe. Others, however, considered the prize as a political manoeuvre rewarding Mahfouz for his positive attitude towards the Egyptian-Israeli peace initiatives. Mahfouz was condemned for his political conservatism rather than for the quality of his work. Finally, Muslim radicals rejected the award as a Western provocation of Islam, celebrating an author who was supposed to have written against religion, particularly against Islam, and presented a distorted image of Egypt's recent history. The prize was seen as a symbol of Western aggression against Islam, supporting atheists, materialists and secularists in the Arab world.

It was not long before Naguib Mahfouz was linked to the more vociferous discussions about the *Satanic Verses* of Salman Rushdie. The association of these two writers is no coincidence, since both have tackled controversial religious issues. The similarities become more visible, however, if one sees their work from the perspective of intercultural exchange between Islamic societies and the West (cf. Pipes, 1990; Ruthven, 1990). It is known that Rushdie considers himself part of at least two cultures, which he melts into a new universe without boundaries and in which traditional cultural identities are transcended. He explicitly fulminates against despots who want to impose their narrow-minded views on culture and who try to define political and cultural boundaries. To illustrate this, he utilises elements from his Islamic-Indian background in a distinctly Western literary form: a novel dealing with identities, metamorphosis and exile (cf. Rushdie, 1991). Thus Rushdie becomes part of at least two cultures, which is where the controversy lies: if a writer lays equal claim to positions in two literatures, then who has the authority to judge the work, to interpret it or to apply the values of his own group on the writer? It is clear that in the case of Rushdie both Western liberals and radical Muslims claimed these rights, drawing Rushdie into their respective cultures.

The award of the Nobel Prize to Naguib Mahfouz had a similar effect. After all, sanctioning of his work by Western cultural patrons not only changed Mahfouz's position in Arabic literature, but it also made him part of Western literature. It meant that, through translation, he would be present in the core of Western culture. This new duality changed the meaning of his work, as it was included into the cultural dialogue between the Arab world and the West. The consequences of his Nobel Prize were that his works had to be reinterpreted according to the new context. The texts had lost their previous meaning, and had to be invested with new meaning by a new dialogic process. This was started by European intellectuals who awarded Mahfouz the prize, thus opening the way for reinterpretation. What ensued, however, was fierce condemnation of his work by some Islamic groups. It was a struggle for the monopoly to judge expressions of culture, to purify the artistic imagination and to appropriate an author in cultures in which the various parties took strong positions.

The cases of Rushdie and Mahfouz are illustrative because they are extreme and seem remote from the daily practice of literary translation. However, they show the essential dilemma involved in the transfer of texts and ideas from one culture to another and the difficulties that confront the translator of Arabic literature. First of all, the two cases resulted in a polarisation within literature, since they forced intellectuals to take sides and to issue public statements. They gave a new polemical relevance to translation and exchange with the West. Translators are often reproached for selecting titles for translation, which are bound to strengthen European prejudices about the Arab world and for refusing to give a balanced picture of the Arabs' cultural heritage. They are accused of seeking financial gain or promoting orientalist biases, appropriating texts to fit their own discourses and endorsing the European foothold in Arab culture. Moreover, they fail to appreciate Arabic literature, as it should be, because of a traditionally depreciative attitude towards Arabs and because of the European monopoly on the formulation of literary standards. Thus translation programmes are often seen as efforts at appropriation and domination rather than exchange.

We have seen above how literary translation became politicised to the extent it now is. In the past, translation was explicitly connected to political relations and to discussions, which touched on the essence of cultural tradition. This is still evident for religious groups, who see literature as an exponent of secularism and a rival regarding the control of culture. Islamists who rail against modern literature have primarily political motives, strengthening the links between culture and politics. But among secularist intellectuals too, there is fear that translation and expansionism go hand in hand and that the false representations of the past are being reproduced uncritically with the aim of cultural domination. Here, too, the inherited symbiosis between culture and politics is of crucial significance. Cultural relations are so intricate and precarious that interference from outside is always looked at with suspicion (cf. Ahmad, 1992).

The problems are derived partly from the different functions of literature in Europe and the Arab world. In Europe, only a few people are aware of the delicate cultural debates and the controversial heritage of the *nahDa* period. Most intellectuals tend to schematise and fall back on stereotyped images when dealing with the debates between secularists and Islamists, and they fail to see how power affects the equilibrium of Arabic literary production. On the other hand, Arab intellectuals are often reluctant to accept that European literature is in essence autonomous and open to the market rather than regulated by the state. Ideologically inspired translation programmes aimed at presenting a faithful survey of Arab-Islamic culture are not likely to appear since they are, firstly, incompatible with the requirements of the book market and, secondly, contrary to intellectual conceptions which would not accept the possibility of such a representation. Selection criteria for translation are inspired by commercial considerations rather than didactic purposes, and programmes to translate texts that are commercially unfeasible usually fail. Misunderstandings such as these are often generated by stereotyped images of the Other, or rigid opinions about each other's societies, and often obscure the real differences in Arab and Western culture.

Conclusion

I have argued in favour of a more flexible and open theoretical framework for analysis of cultural relations between Europe and the Arab world rather than for the still dominant paradigm of orientalism. A rigid, generalising and one-sided model, as conceived by Edward Said, seems unwieldy in the post-colonial era, in which the previous dichotomy between Europe and the Arabs is gradually being replaced by more complex and global cultural relations. Dialogism, as the general source of meaning, and genre, as the structuring principle for knowledge, appear better able to describe the cultural exchange, especially when associated with the notion of interacting cultures in which images of the Other are reproduced and adapted. It is the power relations in which these fields are embedded and the symbolic value of cultural expressions as elements of identity which turn cultural exchange into such a delicate process.

Cultural relations are essential for the translator and for comprehending the difficulties of his or her task. It is even significant for translation itself because here, implicitly, the conventions of the genre, in which images of the Arab world are reproduced, are confirmed and developed. The selection of texts, the style of translation, the reception of translated texts are all related to the interpretative process shaped by the interaction between two literatures, setting the standards for other, future texts. It is not sufficient to say that Arabic literature is systematically being marginalised through unyielding orientalism. It is also too easy to say that texts are translated only to be appropriated by a dominant culture. These approaches deny the dynamism inherent in cultural relationships and in texts themselves, or at least in their interpretation and evaluation.

Furthermore, it is important not to seek the problems connected with translation of Arabic literature solely in Europe. It is an understatement to say that publishing is relatively underdeveloped in the Arab world and that in this regard the European and Arab systems do not fit together smoothly. Cultural repression or difficulties have prompted many authors and journalists to come to European capitals and even to write in European languages. This seems to support fears about europeanisation of Arabic literature but at least in some cases it can be attributed to the cultural climate in the Arab world itself. It shows, though, how much the two literatures have become interconnected and how in both the Other is prominently present. In fact, they cannot escape each other, and the work of translators will remain indispensible for the mutually satisfactory development of existing links.

Chapter 3

Exoticism, Identity and Representation in Western Translation from Arabic

OVIDI CARBONELL

> A bad translation is just a perfect swindle. You pay for reading what the original didn't want to say. You pay for wood riddled with woodworm, you get worm-eaten fruit. And, above all, you pay in order to suffer. I don't know if there's any complaint office out there, but, if there isn't any, it surely should be invented.
>
> (Joan F. Mira, 1999: 114)*

Introduction

A bird's eye view of the major issues in translation (acceptability, preference, equivalence, etc.) shows that deciding between a 'good' or a 'bad' translation cannot be reduced to a series of clear-cut, all-purpose rules. All too often, lectures on translation turn out to be complaint sessions by lecturers striving to provide sound objections to the options students think fit. Error systematisation tends to become a hard task once we need to adopt a wider scope than the usual correction of morpho-syntactic structures. Contrastive rhetorics and stylistics based on corpus analyses offer a secure but still untreaded ground for translation; likewise, it is still early days to assess the significance of cultural studies for translation with regards to the day-to-day need for direction in the didactics and assessment of translation.

Especially when dealing with literary translation of culturally distant cultures and languages, it becomes apparent that there are no easy or consistent solutions: the debate is still centred on the appropiateness of literal versus free approaches. Both translation methods have been used in Spain, for example, in translating Arabic literature, showing diverse results and diverse ways of tackling what seems to be the principal cultural issue:

taking the reader nearer to the source culture or nearer to the target culture. *Foreignising*, that is importing alien elements to the target culture which are supposed to belong to the source culture (for example, by means of loanwords, calques, the discursive structure of the original), is opposed to *familiarising*, a process by which alien elements and their references, that may cause a stranging effect, are reduced to familiar references so that the information of the original is easily understood in terms of the target culture.

To familiarise is to reduce; it tends to imply a reduction in the sense that the complexity of the original context is replaced by a set of relationships inscribed in the target culture's referential universe. In other words, references to realities from the source culture are managed from within the target culture: newness replaced by quotidianeity. The target text may thus be said to enter, as a result of the translation process, into the target culture and to belong there from then on. From within that culture, the reader plays an active role in conferring an acceptable and coherent sense onto the text: the reader 'collaborates' with author and text alike (Eco, 1981). The translator, who is a sophisticated reader of a different kind, collaborates by 'mediating' in the selection of a different linguistic code as well as a different network of cultural references. This does not mean that the translator always substitutes familiar references for foreign ones, which may be the case in certain texts where those references are secondary to the purpose of the translation (e.g. Bible translation), but rather the opposite is true particularly in literary translation from languages such as Arabic where references to alien concepts or customs are usually preserved and somehow clarified in the translated text or explained in footnotes. The point here is that for the reader to interpret in an adequate way what the Arabic text says, it is absolutely necessary that the new information be processed, made to cohere, from inferences taken from the reader's experience and knowledge of the original context. The translator largely prepares the ground for the reader's interpretation, and not merely through a change of linguistic code (translating involves a great deal of cultural transpositions and adaptations). Tackling *newness* always involves an adaptation, a negotiation, the establishment of a common ground or a mediating space. But given that it is difficult to determine the exact nature of such 'personal terrain' (no two interpretations are the same), approaches do change from one culture to another and from one intercultural network to another.

Like the previous chapter, which shows some scepticism about rigid approaches to culture and translation, the aim of this chapter is to argue that considered and applied separately, both linguistic/textual and cultural studies cannot provide adequate and useful assistance in dealing with the complexities of intercultural communication through translation. Drawing on translations from Arabic into Spanish, the case for some exoticism in translating from Arabic may be necessary, for strict dichotomies, foreignisation vs. domestication, for example, do not seem to be flexible enough for either the theorist or the practitioner.

Translation from Arabic

Translating from Arabic into Spanish is paradigmatic in the sense that context setting where interaction takes place is different from that adopted for other languages. Salvador Peña, a Spanish translatologist and translator from Arabic and English, proposes a translation typology organised in terms of the relationship existing between codes:

> We might already draw a distinction between two ways of translating according to the hierarchical or hegemonic relationship that may be established between two or more languages: *glossing*, if we descend down the hierarchical ladder in terms of which languages are thought of in a given social situation (v. gr. translating from English into Spanish); or *deciphering*, in the case we climb up the ladder (v. gr. translating from Arabic into French). (1999: 27)

Deciphering implies something more than the usual instrumental activity of decoding-recoding. It implies a historical fascination for the source code, an attraction to the different ways of codifying thought, but it also reveals the idea that such thought must be itself different and that translation, mainly literary, must somehow convey its difference and strangeness. In translating English into Spanish, for example, any unaccounted for divergence is considered an error, a *woodworm*. But when dealing with translation from Arabic into Spanish or English, or even from Spanish into English, exoticism appears. In fact, and bearing in mind the worm-eaten apples, some people would pay extra for large-size worms in their translations; some would even buy the translation for its worms, especially if these came from Arabic texts. What I have in mind here is the usual literalism or foreignisation that is taken for granted in translations of the *Arabian Nights*, where for example *al-malik as-sa'id* becomes in Spanish ¡Oh rey feliz! (O happy King); although no one would expect a queen to address her husband in such a way, unless that queen is Shahrazad. If bad translations are such because of a difference in adjustment between what the source text and the target text say, then exoticism could be considered an error or a swindle: an ideological device which clarifies a foreign reference in terms of what the target culture expects from the source culture, and not what the latter actually says. It is, in some respects, an inflation of meaning, which is intended as an alleviation of the obvious loss of cultural references, but which in fact replaces some others that occlude, even annul or openly contradict the original ones. This inflation may, however, be necessary to make sense of new realities or experiences.

Translation is a privileged space where linguistic and social systems meet, intermix or come into conflict; the very reason why it has recently received so much attention from cultural studies. But it is not easy to conflate linguistic and social approaches that remain despairingly superficial. Without a discursive, micro dimension, cultural translation theory can only go so far; and without the broad, macro dimension of cultural contact, institutionalisation, hybridisation and the like, purely linguistic and textual approaches to translation remain extremely limited and regarded with suspicion or simply ignored by most cultural theorists.

Although 'the cultural turn' in translation studies has become commonplace, I tend to believe that there is a 'crisis' in cultural translation theory due particularly to: (a) the sheer difficulty in coping with an enormous, largely redundant amount of cultural theory being developed in many fields, and (b) the reticence of cultural translation theorists (and cultural criticism at large) to identify the linguistic mechanisms by which discourse is in the end enacted. Except for a few studies, (Mason, 1995, for example), critical linguistic approaches to translation are few and far between. Exoticism, for example, cannot be explained in terms of functions; functionalist approaches tend to be too rigid and general. What is needed is a semiotic theory that takes into account the pragmatic implications of using socially established images of the Other. Exotic translation generally produces what target readers expect. In the case of Arabic, ethnocentric translators domesticate the literature and its associated culture (see Carbonell, 1997). On this point, Venuti (1998: 83) elaborates:

> A translation project motivated by an ethics of difference thus alters the reproduction of dominant domestic ideologies and institutions that provide a partial representation of foreign cultures and marginalize other domestic constituencies. The translator of such a project, contrary to the notion of 'loyalty' developed by translation theorists like Nord (1991), is prepared to be disloyal to the domestic cultural norms that govern the identity-forming process of translation by calling attention to what they enable and limit, admit and exclude, in the encounter with foreign texts.

But things are by no means so simple: undertaking an ethical project is an almost impossible and perhaps irrelevant task. It may be that there is always a need for the exoticism of the foreign in translation. This is the dimension that translators (and translation theorists) are unable to tackle in a normative and ethical sense. What is worrying is the extreme generalisation underlying concepts such as domestic culture, foreign text or even foreignisation. Translation enables readers to acknowledge, even accept what a priori is an alien text crammed with alien references. Readers make cohere the unfamiliar by accommodating a new system of categories and the human practices they describe or imply. Foreignness is limited. In any given discursive construction (conveyed by a text, a conversation, a series of ad images, a photographic exhibition, etc.) we cannot expect everything to be known or familiar, nor conclude that everything appears to us foreign, alien, odd, or strange. We should instead ask what we understand by known, familiar, foreign or strange. In fact, it is a relatively limited amount of traits that makes a translated text familiar or foreign. Cultural identity may be constructed from a number of semiotic signs. In the case of social or geographic varieties, sociolinguistics tells us that speakers recognise and identify only a few features of language as representative of a particular dialect or social group. Most other traits remain hidden and fluctuant until they generalise enough to become stereotypes.

Similarly, the creation of cultural identities through translation is usually limited to relatively few stereotypes. Few details suffice to distinguish, for example, the speech of a cultured gentleman from that of a peasant. Ethnic differences in translation are usually treated in the same way drawing on the common target culture repertoire of ethnic linguistic stereotypes (when there is a parallel distinction in the target language culture), or else the translator provides substitutes (e.g. Cuban Spanish for Jamaican English as in the movie *The Little Mermaid*).

When literature from so-called exotic cultures is translated, a similar stereotyping process is under way. English or Spanish readers usually classify in advance what they may encounter in a work translated from Arabic, Farsi, Chinese or Malay. That is, they formulate a number of expectations as to the description of the foreign and exotic settings and their categories. So certain themes and discursive features are expected and a specimen of a specific genre is expected: exotic literature. The translator, far from being invisible, usually positions himself/herself before the translated work and intervenes in introductions, glossaries and footnotes. His voice (his subject position) is generally clear in traditional, Romantic or realist exoticism.

The construction of exotic *topoi* (see Karim, 1997; Faiq, this volume) may be enacted by way of phraseology – one of the most important resources of identity production the management of culture-specific items or intertextual references, or the manipulation of subject positions and agency: for example, the use of indirect speech with an omniscient narrator whose interventions complement, control or even replace direct utterances (Carbonell, 2001, 2002). The most apparent of these interventions is the

Orientalist footnote (the translator-as-guide); the least conspicuous is the aside remark or intratextual gloss that attempts a clarification, balance or softening of situations that might be understood as alien. Exotic translations have made literal translations of phraseology one of the main recognisable features of exotic literature as a specific genre. That is, a certain kind of foreignisation is always expected in such ethnocentric translations, so to speak. If we follow Venuti's foreignising advice, we may well reproduce the same strategies we set out to avoid (Carbonell, 1997). Example 1 illustrates how the literalist translation of idiomatic language may be used to reflect the translator's ideological bias.

> 1. El delegado gubernativo se derrumbó en una silla, mientras yo estaba pendiente de sus labios, con mal contenida impaciencia. Pero él se volvió al portero:
> – Tráeme un vaso de agua, por vida de tus ojos.
> Sacó dela manga su pañuelo de seda artificial y se enjugó la car y la cabeza. Yo estaba más que en ascuas. Por fin se volvió a mí y me dijo:
> – Se ha escapado.[1]

> The government's delegate flopped into a chair while I observed his lips with half-contained impatience. But he addressed the porter:
> 'Bring me a glass of water, for the life of your eyes.'
> He took from his sleeve a handkerchief made of synthetic silk and mopped his face and head. I was on tenterhooks. At last he turned to me and said:
> 'She's run away'.

Popular Arabic expressions such as, *waHayaati 'aynayka* (rendered literally into Spanish as *por vida de tus ojos* 'for the life of your eyes') constitute a distinctive trait of the delegate's speech, contrasted with the lawyer's more neutral and standardised speech. The Arab author (al-Hakim) draws therefore a distinction between the language and attitude of both characters: one nearer to the countryside and its way of life; the other to Cairo and European manners. This distinction is articulated in the dichotomies popular vs. urban, underdevelopment vs. progress; both, and this is essential, within the Egyptian cultural framework. In fact, their conflictual aspects lead the reader to believe eventually that the principles and applications of European perspectives may be erroneous. But in offering a literal translation of such idiomatic expressions, the translator adds a new dimension. A new duality appears: East vs. West, only hinted at in the original, but clearly highlighted in the translation. Why not translate pragmatically *¡Tráeme un café, por Dios!* (Bring me a coffee, for God's sake!?)
In another passage, *naharuhu 'aswad* is translated as *¡Negro sea su día!*

'Black be his day!', but a suitable pragmatic rendering such as, ¡*Mal rayo le parta!* or ¡*El diablo le lleve!* 'Damn him!' would have undoubtedly been more appropriate. These exoticisations add something more, and we must recognise that Emilio García Gómez, the translator and also the foremost Spanish Arabist of the 20th century, does discriminate because such foreignisation is *not* a constant in all characters and in all circumstances. The lawyer almost never uses popular expressions: his smooth discourse is no different from the 'usual' in contemporary European fiction, and he is therefore invested with the balanced perspective 'usual' in European realism. The author's voice in the Spanish translation becomes then, through narrator and translator, a trustworthy interpreter of the foreign culture. Spanish stereotypes of Egyptian and Arab backwardness and deviation are confirmed. There is enough evidence for this: the lawyer's use of idiomatic language is always neutralised into functional equivalents. The lawyer speaks with the common sense with which the Spanish, as a Western reader, identifies him/herself. This common sense, as far as it substitutes alternative interpretations, is a rhetorical device that serves ideological purposes.

Example 2 illustrates the critical apparatus that is likely to be found in academic translations from Arabic, in particular, and from distant languages and cultures, in general. In this case, the Lebanese writer Anis Frayha comments on childhood games. In the Spanish translation detailed extra information is given in (4):

2. Difícil me resulta enumerarte nuestros juegos en la plaza del pueblo, en sus callejas, granjas y descampados. Eran muchos y no es fácil, no, enumerarlos. En el fondo de mi mente sólo quedan unos nombres (4): *al-lāqūṭ, daḥw al-kiᶜāb, al-dalak, al-danak, jirŷ al-mallāḥ, maqrᶜat al-maydān, un quq-dos quques, 'Mā brūḥ ṭa-šrab dammū baᶜdu w-ḥayyid li-immū', 'Yā Umm Iskandarānī-Yā Umm ᶜuyūn al-gizlānī', 'Skar kibba ᶜal-markaba', 'Qirriš ¿qaddēš hū?'*, y otros muchos. No creo que sea capaz de describírtelos todos: no recuerdo ahora sus reglas, condiciones y detalles.²

It is difficult for me to list the games we played around in the village square, alleys, farms and open grounds; they were so many it's no easy task to make a list of them. Deep in my mind only a few names remain (4): *al-lāqūṭ, daḥw al-kiᶜāb, al-dalak, al-danak, jirŷ al-mallāḥ, maqrᶜat al-maydān, un quq-dos quques, 'Mā brūḥ ṭa-šrab dammū baᶜdu w-ḥayyid li-immū', 'Yā Umm Iskandarānī-Yā Umm ᶜuyūn al-gizlānī', 'Skar kibba ᶜal-markaba', 'Qirriš ¿qaddēš hū?'*, and many others. I don't think I'll be able to describe all of them to you; I cannot remember their rules, requirements and details.*

(4) El Autor, como dice expresamente un poco más adelante y ha reafirmado en más de una ocasión al preguntársele sobre el tema, no es capaz de describir ni recordar con detalle en qué consistían estos juegos -cuyo origen remoto cree fenicio o siríaco- ni qué significan sus nombres o las letras de las frases en ellos usadas. Por lo tanto, la nomenclatura, explicaciones y equivalencia que a continuación damos son sólo un intento de aproximación de cuya exactitud no podemos responder.

Laqūṭ = Laqūš. Según la descripción del mismo Frayhòa en su Diccionario y las explicaciones de informantes libaneses, es el juego de las *chinas* o una variante del mismo.

Daḥw al-ki-ᶜāb: 'Arrojar los huesecillos o dados'. Según Frayha (ibid.), el *kaᶜb*, plural *kiᶜāb*, son los huesos procedentes de la rodilla del cordero. Los niños juntan unos cuantos y organizan con ellos juegos diversos. Este tipo de juego está muy difundido en Palestina, Siria y el Iraq. Se trata, más o menos, del juego de las *tabas*.

Al-dalak: la fricción (?).

Al-danak: 'caminar imitando el paso de las bestias de carga' (Barth.).

Jirŷ [= clásico *jurŷ*] *al-mallāḥ:* 'la alforja del salinero'. Un chico se pone de gatas y otros dos se cuelgan de él por sus costados, imitando a una montura con sus alforjas.

Maqrᶜat al-maydān: 'el azote o el látigo de la plaza'. *Maqrᶜa:* 'pieza de tela retorcida en forma de cuerda, de la que se sirven los niños como látigo . . . en determinados juegos' (Barth.).

Qūq: Según Barthéleny, 'corneja'. Recoge la letra de una canción que los niños dicen al ver los cuervos.

Ma b-rūh . . . : 'No voy ya a a beber su sangre, porque su madre no tiene más hijos' (?).

Yā Umm al-Iskandarānī . . . : 'Oh señora Iskandarānī, la de ojos de gacela!' (?). Equivale más o menos al juego de la 'pídola'.

Skarkaba o *skar kibba (?):* ignoro qué significa y qué juego designa.

Qirriš . . . : 'Cuenta las piastras: ¿cuántas son?' Es decir, jugar a los chinos.

Readers will certainly be puzzled by the abundance of information which does not add much to their knowledge. The translator himself declares in the footnote (4) that details are irrelevant, so are also the names, the rules, even the nature of the games. The translator has attempted unsuccessfully to furnish the readers with enough anthropological information which is unknown even to average Lebanese, source, readers. What need is there for translating names literally, for example? A functional translation providing probable target-language names, even if their referential value is only conjectural, is all that is pragmatically needed and would be the common procedure in present-day translations from Arabic as performed by the youngest generation of Spanish Arabists.

The profusion of footnotes, the use of complete diacritical marks, make this translation a good example of an academic approach that focuses on difference and underlines the importance of the translator-Orientalist as a necessary expert mediator. Such esoteric added information recalls 19th-century Orientalist translations such as Richard Burton's – whose footnotes largely oversized the translated text – as examined and assessed by Kabbani (1989).

Some post-colonial translators would welcome an extreme foreign-isation that leaves words unglossed, thus enacting a metonymic gap, which should 'represent [the author's] world to the coloniser (and others) in the metropolitan language, and at the same time to signal and emphasise a dif-ference from it' (Ashcroft *et al.*, 2000: 137). This position, not so different from Venuti's, may easily be disfigured when the foreign, opaque word, opens a way for target-culture received stereotypes to substitute source-culture representations.

It is obvious that the foreignising devices in texts 1 and 2 (literal selective translation of phraseology, footnotes, diacritics, etc.) do not counter Western images of its Eastern Others but clearly support them. Such tradi-tional, academic foreignising could be dubbed a case of domestication, for Venuti's dichotomy does not seem to be so clear as regards translation of Arabic literature into Spanish. It is equally not clear whether a minoritising translation strategy should apply to a pair of languages the translations of which are 'minority' anyway. The true minoritising project here would imply to assimilate Arabic translation to the mainstream translation market.

I am not sceptical about minoritising translation projects, and Venuti's, in particular, rather I do not entirely agree with Venuti's excessive, general and normative approach that may work in certain ways but is hard to extrapolate to different circumstances and which does not take into account the different status of languages and texts – nor even the very nature of language. Nevertheless, I agree that translation, a complex dis-cursive process largely based on representation, plays and should play a part in the deconstruction of received images and stereotypes. The intersti-tial, overlapping nature of cultural translation should provide examples of the instability and ambivalence theorised by cultural critics such as Homi Bhabha and Gayatri Spivak – but conscious foreignising projects seem to provide a neoexoticist, institutionalising status to texts which modify or even replace the original representations and categories. Of course, any translation or act of communication modifies the original construction, but this modification requires an in-depth discursive analysis that might lead to consistent normative 'recommendations.'

One of the inherent difficulties of partial analysis (and resulting normative advice) is a failure to view cultural translation as a multidirectional process. For example, post-colonial writers may well play with usual (Western) exotic stereotypes. Should we regard post-colonial works as _exceptions_ to the general dichotomies of East vs. West or even source culture vs. target culture? Consider example 3.

> 3. _Kan ma kan/ Fi qadim azzaman_ . . . Tal vez sí o tal vez no, vivían en tiempos remotos en la tierra de la plata de la Argentina un tal don Enrique Diamond . . . [3]

Here, Salman Rushdie starts a chapter with a transliteration of the usual phrase found in Arabic folktales followed by a literal translation. No further explanation, note or glossary explains the meaning of the initial phrases. There is, however, a literary convention by which a foreign phrase is sometimes introduced followed by its translation. The first Spanish (or English, in the original) words produce an unusual beginning: _Tal vez sí o tal vez no_ . . . , followed by the usual cliché that announces the beginning of a tale: . . . _vivían en tiempos remotos_. One would have expected instead the hackneyed _Había una vez_ . . . or _Hace mucho tiempo_ . . . 'Once upon a time . . . ' The reader infers successfully, although s/he is unable to check this, that this unusual beginning corresponds word-for-word with the foreign introductory formula of a tale, probably in Arabic or similar Oriental language: Urdu or Hindi. As there exists a literalist and exoticising tradition at work in the translation of oriental texts, readers find themselves prepared to encounter oddly constructed phrases or certain images of rhetorical figures which in other contexts would be inappropriate. Compare Rushdie's use of the expression with Inea Bushnaq's (1986: xvi) explanation drawing on exotic topics, but delving into her own experience:

> _Kan ma kan._ 'There was, there was not.' To an Arab the words evoke memories of winter evenings with a roomful of women stitching, their tired servants and sleepy children held in thrall by an old lady whispering of giants with teeth of silver and teeth of brass, of princesses like cypress trees whose brows shine clear as the Pleiades, of lovelorn heroes pale as the crocus ailing for the affection of such princesses. Or they might conjure up the endless hot nights when Ramadan falls in the summer [. . .].

It is a distinctive feature of literature that there may exist several levels of interpretation from which the reader obtains coherent readings. Inferences are done at a rather superficial level; readers go on reading 'in suspense' until further confirmation of their conjectures (see Van Dijk & Kintsch, 1983). Any reader knowledgeable in Arabic language or literature would have noticed that *kan ma kan* is a typical introductory phrase of a tale, therefore concluding that Rushdie wishes to draw a parallel between popular folkloric narrative and the story he is about to transmit. It is a case of 'weak information' that the author did not want to make explicit for his English language readers, in the original work. Should the translator clarify this reference, for example, with a note? Rushdie himself provides a literal translation that the Spanish translator respects (*Tal vez sí o tal vez no*, instead of *Érase que se era* or *Había una vez*) and which gives a sense of indeterminacy, a key concept in Rushdie's thought. Any similar case should be contrasted bearing in mind the intended effect (Hatim & Mason, 1990) on readers of the original text. Here the author clearly wants a veiled reference, a quote from a code largely unknown to the target language readers, and the translator accurately reproduces the obscurity of the original.

The example also shows that exotic *topoi* are fundamental to the understanding of the author's intentions and in the articulation of a strategy for cultural translation. A functional rendering like *Había una vez; Érase que se era* 'once upon a time' would neutralise the author's pragmatic, intertextual and semiotic elaboration. We might therefore agree here with Venuti's foreignising proposals, but we should also acknowledge that *it was the author, not the translator*, who prompted the foreignising move in the first place.

It is obvious that global tendencies provide the terrain for similar negotiations and interplays of cultural differences and signs of identity. Twenty-first century Arab authors, for example, are quite aware of European imaginaries of the Orient and sometimes deal with them in their works, providing translators with an ambiguous space of negotiation that quite often forces readers and translators alike to question their own assumptions and cultural identifications. The translator may as well neutralise such an ambiguous, 'in-between' space (Bhabha, 1994); but it is my contention that it is by way of stereotypical foreignisation that neutralisation (domestication) takes place, at least as regards exotic literature.

4. La palmera solitaria del patio terroso evoca un cementerio. Lo piensa mientras lo cruza camino de la puerta de la calle. El casero, que regaba el suelo con la manguera, le interceptó el paso [. . .][4]

The lonely palm-tree in the earthy yard evokes a cemetery. He thinks about it while crossing the yard towards the street door. The landlord, who had been hosing down the ground, stood in front of him and barred his way [. . .]

5. Dhahabtu ilà al-Iskandariyya ꜥabra aṭ-ṭarīq aṣ-ṣaḥrāwī. Uḥhibbuhu akthar min aṭ-ṭarīq az-zirāꜥī alladhī yamurru ꜥabra quran wa bilād ad-daltā ar-ratībati al-mawkhamati.[5]

Fui a Alejandría por la carretera del desierto. La prefiero a la de la campiña, que cruza por los pueblos y por los terrenos monótonos e insalubres del Delta.

I travelled to Alexandria through the desert road. I prefer it to the fields road, which goes through the villages and the monotonous, unhealthy lands of the Delta.

Text samples 4 and 5 provide the reader with a feeling of disquiet, which springs from the unexpected connotations of known cultural realities. In 4, the Spanish language reader would have expected a cypress tree evoking a cemetery atmosphere and not a palm tree, which is usually associated with Mediterranean landscapes, charm and ease of life, the opposite of all macabre or dreadful. This feeling is unavoidable, depending on the characteristics of the setting that the reader must assume. Similarly, *campiña* 'countryside, fields', in 5, has positive connotations and is associated with green, luscious landscapes (*la campiña inglesa*), not normally with the orchard landscape one finds in the Nile Delta. While in accordance with the author's seemingly incongruous preference for a desolated road, the translator's option reverses, deconstructs or even *interrupts* (Bhabha, 1994: 136) what we may call the traditional orientalist/exotic discourse, thus helping build an analogy between the (Spanish) Same, Us and the (Arab) Other. This I consider to be a type of 'subversive familiarisation.'

The samples show a stranging effect that helps the reader locate the action of the text in order to build an alternative reality, which may or may not be subject to the same rules the reader is familiar with. If substituting cypress for palm tree would impair such an alternative world and be utterly incongruous, its preservation does nevertheless widen the target reader's experience and help them be receptive to the society reflected in the source text. Such examples further indicate that in any translation, even the most literalist and foreignising, the familiar still has a far from negligible role (coherence would not be possible otherwise) in order to construct epistemologically a coherent account (cf. Potter, 1996). We should not overlook the role of familiarisation, which is overwhelmingly prevalent in translation, as the necessary process that enables the creation of new identities.

Conclusion

Fidelity to the source culture, whatever the definition adopted, poses difficult ethical questions. Whenever there is a noticeable cultural gap, ideological choices constantly torment translators and determine their choices. A coherent, decolonising agenda should be directed to induce an 'awareness of the subject positions that inhabit any claim to identity in the modern world' (Bhabha, 1994: 1). This awareness unavoidably leads to the coexistence of conflicting ideological structures or representational models. Translators can be trained to develop such awareness and produce ambivalent, 'hyphenated' descriptions with a social role, but their translations will in no way be devoid of exotic implications. Although limited in scope, this chapter has tried to show that in addition to current linguistic / textual and cultural studies, the fundamental aspects of the assimilation and articulation of new realities through translation require cognitive and discursive research. Four points summarise the discussion in this chapter:

(1) Exoticising ideologies in translation should be analysed through an interdisciplinary approach combining semiotics, discourse analysis and cultural criticism.
(2) Domestication/ foreignising is a confusing and simplistic dichotomy.
(3) Literary translations from so-called exotic cultures often resort to literalist foreignising to prop up exotic, ethnocentric stereotypes.
(4) Minoritising translation strategies are fairly difficult to control and may produce undesirable results

Those who praise the virtues of intercultural exchange and multiculturalism may forget that any approach to the Other responds to the intrinsic need to know and dominate through knowledge, or the need to overcome in a vicarious way the anxious and unbearable feeling of decentring, fragmentation and insecurity imposed by certain cultural modes at the turn of the century. We should reflect, as Eagleton (1991) does, whether 'difference, hybridation, heterogeneity and restless mobility' are not a consequence of the substitution of a producer subject who is 'mobile, ephemeral and determined by insatiable desire'. In fact, I am of the opinion that, at least as regards Western contemporary exoticism, there *is* a desire for otherness in the form of ethnic or hybrid oriental texts or cultural artefacts (the *other*, the different that is not so different but were it not because this difference would pass unnoticed). All these are of course commodities. Hybridisation is only apparent from the moment we look, read, buy and close the hybrid subject as an abstraction that is no more than yet another variant of our construction of the other in opposition to the construction of ourselves.

Notes
* Unless otherwise indicated, all translations into English are mine.
1. al-Hakim, Tawfiq (1987) *Diario de un fiscal rural* (trans. Emilio García Gómez). Madrid: IHAC (pp. 79-80).

2. Frayha, Anis (1978) *Escucha, Rida.* (trans. J.M. Fórneas). Madrid: IHAC (pp. 213–14)
3. Rushdie, Salman (1989) *Los versos satánicos* (trans. J.L. Miranda). Madrid: Varias Editoriales (p. 143).
4. Mahfuz, Naguib (1974) 'El sueño' (*Cuentos ciertos e inciertos,* trans. Marcelino Villegas y María Jesús Viguera). Madrid: IHAC (p.163).
5. Masaad, Raouf (1994) *Bayd 'an-na'aama.* London: Riad El-Rayyes Books (pp. 96–7). (Spanish translation: Salvador Peña, published as Basta, Raúf M. (1997) *El huevo del avestruz.* Guadarrama: Ediciones del Oriente y del Mediterráneo (p. 106).

Chapter 4

Autobiography, Modernity and Translation

TETZ ROOKE

Introduction

It has often been remarked that the Arabic novel shows a strong auto-biographical tendency, especially during the first phase of its development in Egypt in the 1920s and 1930s. A traditional explanation is that the autobiographical novel represents an easier, indeed more 'primitive', form of novel writing, mostly adopted by inexperienced writers who have not yet mastered the art of the novel (Jad, 1983: 42; Kilpatrick, 1974: 155–6). But if the autobiographical nature of early Arab experiments in novel writing, like *Zaynab* (1913) by Muhammad Husayn Haykal, *yawmiyyaat naa'ib fi l-aryaaf* (*The Diary of a District Attorney*, 1937) and *'usfuur min ash-sharq* (*Bird of the East*, 1938) by Tawfiq al-Hakim, and *Ibrahim al-kaatib* (*Ibrahim the Writer*, 1931) by Ibrahim al-Mazini, to name some standard examples, is seen as a sign of inexperience and lack of literary craftsmanship, how then are we to explain the prominence of autobiographical elements in the advanced and sophisticated novels of later generations of Arab writers? In texts by Jabra Ibrahim Jabra, for example, or Edwar al-Kharrat, or Aliya Mamdouh, Ghada Samman and many other talented contemporary women writers? Are the Arab novelists eternal *beginners*? Of course not. Hence we must drop the view that the autobiographical plot represents a simpler form of novel than other types. Admittedly, early Arabic novels have their artistic flaws, but the hero's often close resemblance to the author is not one of them. World literature is full of examples of splendid novels that are also autobiographical and by no means simple. Suffice it here to mention Marcel Proust and *A la rechèrche du temps perdu*.

So what is a better explanation? Stephan Guth (1998) suggests that the secret of the autobiographical novel in Arabic literature, until the early

1970s, is 'the need for self-protection'. In the case of male writers this is to protect their dignity, their *sharaf,* by avoiding being too personal, and in the case of women writers to protect themselves from attacks because they were penetrating the public (male) sphere of society. His surprising assumption is that, if the Arab writers had not felt this need for self-protection, they would have written instead explicit, straightforward auto-biographies or autobiographical sketches!

The close identity of author and hero/heroine is not, therefore, a result of imperfect knowledge of the art of fiction. On the contrary, the popularity of the autobiographical plot is the sign of a most conscious effort on the part of the Arab writer to explore and lay bare the remains of his or her own private past. For social reasons, however, this could not be done in total transparency.

But why this collective urge to write the (hi)story of oneself, be it presented as a novel or an undisguised autobiography? For the period in question, Guth proposes 'urgent psychological need' due to rapid social change and conflicting life patterns (rural-urban, traditional-modern, Western-Oriental) as the answer. After 1970, Guth continues, the increasing number of Arabic novels with plots grafted on the author's biography and personal experiences has to do with a general subjective tendency in art (as a reaction to a previous dominant social realist one). The inner universe is the only 'authentic' source of knowledge once the lies of official propaganda and totalitarian ideology have become apparent. The authors now employ autobiographical elements as a means to question the dominant order and expose the failures of society. The tale of their own personal disappointments in life has a symbolic function, and they prefer to tell it as fiction instead of straightforward autobiography mainly to enhance the generality of their private case.

On this last point I must disagree with Guth, firstly because autobiography proper also became increasingly popular as a literary genre during the period he analyses, and secondly because the 'truth' of conventional auto-biographies is no less symbolic than that of autobiographical novels. Great autobiographies are appreciated without reference to the actual lives and works of the authors; the specific dynamic truth of autobiography emerges from the text itself, he says, and is identical with the emotional and symbolic truth of art, as opposed to the (supposedly) factual and neutral truth of the document, and where the self that is at the centre of all autobiographical narrative is necessarily a fictive structure. Moreover, literary historians and critics regularly read books of autobiography as symbolic representations of the consciousness of whole communities or even entire peoples. The American theorist James Olney even regards autobiographical writing as a privileged source of knowledge about foreign culture, be it the foreign culture of an individual, a smaller group or a whole society (Olney, 1973, 1980): 'Autobiography renders in a peculiarly direct and faithful way the experience and the vision of a people, which is the same vision lying behind and informing all the literature of that people' (Olney, 1980: 13).

In Arabic literature Jacques Berque (1995: 367) finds in *al-Ayyaam* (*The Days*, 3 vols 1929, 1939, 1967), the noted autobiography by the blind Egyptian writer and reformer Taha Hussein, a story about a whole people's difficult path from darkness to rationality. Drawing on recent thinking about autobiography as a minority expression, Susanne Enderwitz (1998a, 1998b) and Robin Ostle (1998) both point to how Palestinian autobiography shares in the process of creating a collective memory for the Palestinian people. Burgi Ross (1996) interprets along similar lines the poetic childhood autobiography *al-Jundub al-Hadiidi* (*The Iron Grasshopper*, 1980) and its sequel *Hatih 'aliya* (*Play the Trumpet High*, 1982) by the Syrian-Kurdish writer Salim Barakat as a symbolic discourse on behalf of the whole Kurdish nation. The examples could be multiplied, but it seems evident that the autobiographer's choice between fictional or factual narrative approach to his subject need not be dictated by the demands of representativity or generality. Other factors, some of which I have discussed elsewhere (Rooke, 1997: 40–51), are just as important.

But this apart, just like Guth, I believe that the popularity of the Arabic autobiographical novel (and by extension personal account literature in general) has psychological causes that may be understood as reactions to social development. It is wrong to reduce the Arab writers' continuous fondness of autobiographical narratives to a matter of lacking literary skill or experience. In this chapter I will try to boil down these different psychological causes to one common theme of unbroken importance during the 20th century. I will argue that the autobiographical character of much of modern Arabic literature, across all genres, both fiction and non-fiction, is tied to a typical project of modern man, namely the quest for identity. Further, I propose that this quest for identity unites Arabs and 'Westerners' and overarches cultural differences between them. Any text that success-fully addresses the 'problem' of the individual and his or her relation to society and its norms and values is of universal interest. In my view transla-tions of contemporary Arabic personal account literature into European languages demonstrates this affinity between the two, discursively estranged, 'worlds' and may function as a bridge between them. This idea also informs a current international translation programme, *Mémoires de la Méditerranée*, the activities of which will be presented in the second part of my discussion.

The Quest for Identity

According to the sociologist Zygmunt Bauman, the quest for identity is the most characteristic feature of both modern and post-modern society. Men and women everywhere are obsessed with identity because modernity invented identity as a problematic concept. Modern society formed individuals no longer sure of their belonging, who experienced a sense of social 'free-floatingness' that created a need to think about one's identity, or lack of it:

> One thinks of identity whenever one is not sure where one belongs; that is, one is not sure how to place oneself among the evident variety of behavioural styles and patterns, and how to make sure that people around would accept this placement as right and proper, so that both sides would know how to go on in each other's presence. 'Identity' is a name given to the escape sought from that uncertainty. (Bauman, 1996: 19)

From this perspective Arab society entered modernity a long time ago. The dramatic social changes that took place in the Arab world over the last century very early on produced a feeling of uncertainty of belonging that made many Arabs think about their identity. Naturally this did not happen everywhere at once. Some countries or areas became modern before others. Life in Egypt changed before it did so in the interior of Arabia, and big cities were socially and mentally transformed before small villages. I would love to use Arabic autobiographies to evidence this statement, because they give such a vivid image of the process, but in order to avoid a circular argument I will pick my examples from other sources. Richard van Leeuwen (1998b: 28) notes that in the Arab world the question of identity came to the fore especially in the 19th century, when European penetration in economic, military and political fields increased and traditional outlooks came under strain. In his study of Egyptian history between 1880 and 1952, Jacques Berque (1995) gives an excellent description of what happened. Through the impact of British occupation and imperialism, the Egytian economy was fundamentally transformed and 'globalised'. Extensive cultivation of export crops like cotton and sugar cane became a source of national wealth, but also made the country into a servant and client to international capital. Enormous profits were made by the rich at the same time as misery grew among the poor. Thus the average real income in 1950 was only 70% of what it had been in 1913 (Berque, 1995: 648). Along with the economic penetration, an intensified cultural exchange with Europe took place that challenged traditional self-awareness.

Urbanisation visibly transformed both the human and physical landscape. Alexandria, for example, expanded from a sleepy small town to a Mediterranean metropolis. Cairo too boomed, and there the clash between the inherited style and the functions of modernity was sometimes violent. As early as 1881 a committee for the preservation of the cultural heritage was formed to counter the city planners' attempt to tear down old buildings, straighten out the streets and remove all irregularities; geometric thinking collided with aesthetic in a symbolic identity conflict typical of modern society. Production and consumer patterns in the cities changed and new groups of professionals emerged, like journalists, engineers, doctors and lawyers, to name a few. A certain industrialisation took place and a new class of workers was formed.

The inner landscape was also radically transformed. Berques' book abounds in examples, from different periods, of expressions of uncertainty and the quest for roots. I will restrict myself to one. Around 1950 the most popular topics in the Egyptian debate were: moral decay, weakening of the family, drug abuse, different types of escape (suicide included) crime and corruption. Confusion, frustration and anxiety were the key words in discussions of the time (Berque, 1995: 676). It all sounds very, very familiar.

On the basis of this evidence we may well define 20th-century Arab society as a *modern society*, although technologically and economically under-developed and exploited, and not as a traditional one. Such an understanding of modernity challenges the epistemology and world-view of the Arab *nahDa* movement (coloured by European colonial discourse) that produced a theory of modernisation, which *a priori* stated that Arab society was backward and hopelessly non-modern. But by adopting a different view we understand why autobiography in a wide sense is so important in modern Arabic literature. It is modernity itself which is the reason why the autobiographical tendency has proved resistant to all political changes and ideological trends, why it has been followed by devout Muslims as well as secular libertines, by both experienced and inexperienced writers, and has come to permeate many different genres under different political periods and in different national contexts.

Along these lines Saree Makdisi (1995) argues that we must dissociate Arab modernity, as an already existing condition, from modernisation as the dominant – but failed – political and intellectual project since the beginning of the *nahDa*. Modernisation has failed because by definition it cannot be achieved. It is always a project and never a stage. The modernity that is the goal of modernisation can never materialise, because it always exists as an imagined future. It always has to be somewhere else (very much like identity). Thus Makdisi wants us to understand modernity in the Arab world of today as a forever incomplete mixture of various scales and 'stages' of development, as a forever incomplete mixture of styles, forms, narratives, and tropes, as a process whose 'completion' implies and involves a continuous lack of completion. (Makdisi, 1995: 111)

If Arab society in this sense has been modern for a long time it must also for a long time have experienced the problem about identity which accompanies modernity. Indeed, summing up Arab culture in a few words, Jacques Berque (1978: 238) has concluded that 'the quest for self (country as self, people as self, history as self) constitutes one of the most prominent sectors of contemporary Arab production'. 'Self' may here be understood as a synonym of 'identity', and in literature there are few genres more directly related to the quest for self/identity than autobiography 'the history of one's own life'. As van Leeuwen (1998b: 27) puts it, 'the practice of autobiography is essentially an effort to conceive, confirm or stress a certain sense of identity'. This way the autobiographical text can validly be interpreted as the attempt of the writer to create his/her own identity (self) in the present of writing, but at the same time it also reads as the story of the same project, the creation/conformation/stressing of the author's identity in the historical past.

To sum up: modern society generates an uncertainty of belonging in the individual. This uncertainty makes him or her reflect on identity, and autobiography is the direct artistic expression of this self-reflection. Therefore modernity can be said to be the historical condition that explains why so many contemporary literary texts in Arabic have a strong autobiographical dimension.

A Cultural Bridge

Arab modernity has coexisted with Western modernity (now postmodernity) for a relatively long time. For the same reasons as those outlined above autobiographical novels, autobiography proper, memoirs, diaries and similar genres are also very popular in Europe and the USA. This means that corresponding literary practices unite the different cultures. But can this stereographic rendering of the common identity problem also be received and appreciated as such by the public? What is the potential of autobiography to bridge the cultural gap(s)?

If the quest for identity is a shared dilemma then any contemporary text exploring this theme ought to have the potential to attract any modern reader irrespective of cultural background. Why should cultural differences (imagined or real) between writer and reader be more problematic than other differences, such as gender, class or generation? On the contrary, it seems to me that autobiographical narratives like no other stories have the power to bridge cultural differences through their focus on the individual. They highlight the fact that modern cultures are not homogeneous, nor bounded in space. The most common cultural clashes do not take place on the map but in the street. Today Arab culture is a part of Western culture as much as Western culture is a part of Arab culture. If artistically successful and genuine, autobiographical writing is able to give the reader a chance to meet the cultural Other not as psychologically different but same, not as intellectually inferior but equal, and deconstruct the cultural barriers.

This idea comes from personal experience as a reader, but is also supported by critics and writers. In a study of Arabic autobiography, the Egyptian scholar Abdul Aziz Sharaf claims that interpersonal communication is a major function of the autobiographical text. Autobiography stimulates and nurtures an empathic capacity in the reader to identify with other people's fate and arguments (Sharaf, 1992: 75, 82–3, 132–3). The philosopher Martha Nussbaum refers, in a different context, to this kind of empathic capacity as 'narrative imagination' and deems it vital to positive development in today's multi-cultural societies (cf. Ambjörsson, 1999).

As an example of an Arab writer who also believes that the message of autobiography is able to break barriers, presumably also cultural ones, we may take the Egyptian novelist Ibrahim al-Mazini (1890–1949). In the introduction to his autobiography *Qissat Haya* (*The Story of a Life*, 1943), he explains that his serious self-analysis in this text has a didactic purpose, because exposing oneself publicly means teaching others to recognise and discover themselves as human beings. Differences in wealth, upbringing and appearance do not change the fact that human experience essentially is the same for all of us (al-Mazini, 1971: 8–9).

European autobiographies often have been read and appreciated along these lines by an Arab audience, which has looked to the Other to search for the Self. The opposite, however, is not so true, namely that the European reader has not enjoyed an Arabic autobiographical text for its ability to formulate the common identity problem in an original and thought-provoking way.

The first and obvious reason for this imbalance is that many Arabs know European languages well, but very few Europeans are able to read Arabic. When it comes to translations, Arabic autobiography is a neglected field, while Western life-stories are available in Arabic in a comparatively greater number. The second reason is the prejudice of the European audience. The dominant images of the Arab cultural Other in Europe are stereotyped clichés, either exotic and romanticising (the wise sufi, the noble Beduin, the sexy belly-dancer, etc.), hostile and demonising (the political extremist, the backward peasant, the cruel husband, the ruthless dictator, etc.) or patronising and victimising (the poor beggar, the helpless refugee, the suppressed wife, etc.). To many Europeans these images have come to define *Arabness*, although most Arabs refuse to be identified with any one of them.

Challenging the Clichés

Translation of Arabic literature is one way to challenge the clichés and promote better understanding of Arab society and culture today. Because of their transcultural relevance and appeal, autobiographical texts may serve this purpose better than other texts. These are also the fundamental assumptions behind a new European programme for the translation and publishing of contemporary Arabic literature called *Mémoires de la Méditerranée*, set up in 1994. The initiators were two internationally known Arabists and translators, Yves-Gonzalez Quijano (French) and Hartmut Fähndrich (German). Forming a network presently consisting of nine 'correspondents', of whom the author of this chapter is one, representing nine different European languages, this group has been involved in the slow process of building interest in contemporary Arabic literature in their different national literary communities. So far the focus has been on non-fictional life-stories and texts with an autobiographical dimension.

Traditionally translation of texts of this type has been a concern for academic scholarship only and not aimed at a wider audience. Typical examples in English are the translations of autobiographies by Arab intellectuals like Ahmad Amin (*My Life*, 1978), Salama Musa (*The Education of Salama Musa*, 1961) and Muhammad Kurd Ali (*The Memoirs of Muhammad Kurd Ali*, 1956). In this academic tradition of translation, the text is chosen primarily for its documentary value and historical interest. The implied reader is the Western Orientalist.

The *Mémoires de la Méditerranée* programme represents a different approach. Here too the books are selected according to documentary value, but even more important is their literary or aesthetic value and possible commercial potential. Each title must be able to attract a publisher willing to invest in the book and promote it on the commercial market. The implied reader is the general reader and not the specialist. The institutional basis for the programme is a non-profit cultural foundation in Amsterdam, the European Cultural Foundation, that offers financial support to the publisher for 60% of the translation costs and an advance of the royalties to the author, but the rest of the costs have to be met by the publisher as in any other business enterprise.

An example of work that combines documentary value, literary quality and commercial potential is a text by a leading contemporary Arab novelist, Abdul Rahman Mounif. In *siirat madina* (*Story of a City*, 1994) he narrates his childhood memories from the 1940s. He does it as a twin story about personal growth and development and about urban growth and development of the surrounding city of Amman. The boy-protagonist is depicted at the start of an identity building process, his creation of himself, and so is the Jordanian capital whose lack of historical roots and quest for identity makes it a perfect metaphor of Arab modernity and uncertainty about belonging.

The first achievement of the *Mémoires*-programme is a series of quality translations of contemporary literary works that otherwise would probably have remained unavailable to European readers. Currently, nine Arabic titles have been translated and over 30 books have appeared. A unique feature is the coordination in time: all the translations of the same work appear more or less simultaneously in the different languages. For example, *Story of a City* appeared in seven languages in 1996. Most other works have not reached the same number, but *'aziizi as-sayyid Kawabata* (*Dear Mister Kawabata*, 1995) by the Lebanese novelist Rashid al-Daif set a record with eight translations when it was published in Dutch, English, French, German, Italian, Polish, Spanish and Swedish in the winter of 1998–1999.

The series includes both internationally respected Arab writers and less well-known names, like the historian Khaled Ziyadeh, who describes his childhood in Tripoli in the north of Lebanon during the 1950s and 1960s in *Yawm al-jum'a, yawm al-'aHad* (*Friday, Sunday*, 1994). Palestinian identity is reflected in *Dhakira li nisyan* (*Memory for Forgetfulness*, 1985) by the poet Mahmoud Darwish and *al-Bi'r al-'uula* (*The First Well*, 1986) by Jabra Ibrahim Jabra. The personal experience of women is narrated in *Hamlat taftish* (*The Search*, 1992) by Latifa Zayyat, an Egyptian writer, feminist and political activist, and by Aliya Mamdouh in *Habbat naftaliin* (Mothballs, 1986) from Baghdad. Together these writers portray daily life in different parts of the Arab world, but also in some cases Europe, from the point of view of the immigrant, like Raouf Musad-Basta in *bayDat n-na'aama* (*The Ostrich Egg*, 1994) or Abdelkader al-Jannabi in *tarbiyat al-Jannabi* (*The Education of al-Jannabi*, 1995).

This corpus offers interesting material for comparative studies on how Arabic can be rendered in different target languages, although the translators have sometimes cooperated with each other in finding solutions to translation problems. A regular feature of the *Mémoires*- programme has been the organisation of translation workshops where the translators meet for a few days to discuss textual and translation issues with the Arab author whose work has been chosen. These workshops have been held in cooperation with the School of Translators in Toledo, Spain.

However, influence from existing translations may be a factor behind other translations, too. It is the direct cooperation which is different here; a common workshop with the author and perhaps internal circulation of drafts. But from my own experience of the workshops I know that each translator keeps both his/her individual approach to the source text and also a personal strategy for rendition into his/her native language. Close cooperation with the author reduces the scope for mistakes and harmonises the understanding of the text to some extent, but it does not spoil the artistic integrity of the translators or the stylistic diversity of their translations.

The Impact

Despite its literary merits and general interest, Arabic autobiography has not been widely translated. Autobiographical texts have been translated now and again, especially into major languages like English, French and German where the number of Arabic literary works in translation is fairly large, but they have not been translated systematically. What the *Mémoires de la Méditerranée* can do is strengthen this type of literature in the translated corpus. In other languages, like Spanish and Italian, the impact of a programme such as this could be greater; and even more so in a small language such as Swedish where translation from Arabic is weak. There are only approximately 45 literary works in Swedish translated from Arabic, including both classical and modern texts. There was a translation boom after Naguib Mahfouz received the Nobel Prize for literature in 1988, but since 1994 very few Arabic works have been translated and the introduction of new names has proven virtually impossible (Stagh, 1998). Presently in Sweden translations from English completely dominate the book market. According to official statistics in 1997 there were 822 translations of fiction from English, but not a single one from Arabic (Bjärvall, 1998). In such a situation the translation of even one or two books from Arabic is something culturally positive and noteworthy. In addition, such translations provide an opportunity for new translators to gain experience and establish themselves professionally. The circle of Swedish translators from Arabic is limited, which has frequently led to translations from second languages in the case of certain Arabic titles, with all the distortions of the source text that this entails.

Conclusion

I have argued that the strong autobiographical tendency in modern Arabic prose should be explained as a literary response to modernity, because modernity is characterised by the quest for identity, which is the cardinal subject of autobiography. Since modernity is a global phenomenon that already came to (parts of) the Arab world a hundred years ago, the individual's uncertainty about his or her belonging has been a shared problem for both Arabs and Europeans for a long time. Therefore I propose that autobiographical texts can narrow the cultural divide that politics and propaganda have constructed to separate them. To the European reader the discovery of a shared, subjective experience may create a deeper understanding of the different objective conditions, of what they comprise and mean and do not mean. This in turn offers special possibilities for translation as a way of challenging the dominant clichés of *Arabness*. It is possible that the *Mémoires de la Méditerranée* translation and publishing project run by the European Cultural Foundation will go some way to remove the deficit in translated Arabic works, at least as far as European languages are concerned. In this way translation can span the imagined cultural divide and de-mystify the Arab mind to European readers.

Chapter 5

Integrating Arab Culture into Israeli Identity through Literary Translations from Arabic into Hebrew

HANNAH AMIT-KOCHAVI

Introduction

Since the advent of the Zionist movement in the Middle East, the Jewish community in Palestine and later the state of Israel has been an isolated Hebrew-speaking enclave in the Arabic-speaking Middle East. Military conflict between Jews and Arabs has been accompanied by cultural conflict. However, throughout the 134 years (1868–2002) under discussion here, there have been some notable exceptions – there have been Jews familiar with Arabic language and culture, as well as Arabs with a good command of Hebrew, who sought to bridge the cultural gap between Jews and Arabs both to try to solve the political conflict between them and to resolve questions of their own identity. Translating Arabic literature into Hebrew was one of their main tools, and this chapter aims to highlight the background of some translators and illustrate what they sought to achieve. The period under discussion will cover the history of those translations I have traced from 1868, earlier than the first Zionist immigration (1882), up to 2002, when Israel and the Middle East have been involved in a complex peace process as well as renewed bloody conflicts.

The key word here is *identity*. The question of identity has repeatedly troubled various groups of Israelis, and translations of Arabic literature into Hebrew have provided it with different answers at different points in history. The crystallisation of identity has always taken place *vis-à-vis* the Other, the Arab, who served as a reflection of both difference and similarity, evoking a variety of conflicting emotions such as admiration and attraction, on the one hand, and fear, hatred and disdain, on the other (see Amit-Kochavi, 1996, 2000).

Israeli Jewish culture portrayed the Arab through a number of stereotypes predominant in Hebrew literature (Domb, 1982; Friedlander, 1989; Ramraus-Rauch, 1989) and drama (Urian, 1996) as well as in Israeli art (Zalmona and Manor-Friedman, 1998), dance (Eshel, 1991), music (Bahat, 1972; Asaf, 1984) and cinema (Schnitzer, 1994). Most of these stereotypes have persisted throughout the period under discussion. This chapter describes four case studies that illustrate how different groups have made use of literary translation from Arabic into Hebrew to try to balance the Jewish (or Israeli) and Arab sides of their respective identities.

Back to the Biblical Homeland: The Arab as Reminiscent of the Past and a Model for the Present

The first portrayal of the Arab was made by the earliest Jewish immigrants to Palestine. These were East European Jews seeking not only to return to their historical homeland but also to revive the Jewish people which they considered as weakened by centuries of living in the diaspora. Revival meant drastic change – from being merchants and scholars to doing physical labour, from living in crowded and secluded neighbourhoods to living among nature, from being persecuted by the Gentiles, unable to defend themselves, to becoming fighters who knew how to use weapons (cf. Eisenstadt, 1954).

These idealists came to Palestine from Europe and found a harsh hot climate and hard work. In order to adjust they imitated the Arabs, the inhabitants of Palestine who knew how to live there (Even Zohar, 1990: 175–191). Jews wore Arab clothes, the *ibba* and *kufiyya*. They learned how to bake Arab bread in the *tabuun* and eat olives and olive oil. Some of them learned how to use a gun and a knife, the *shibriyya*. They borrowed Arab melodies for their new shepherd and fighter songs and danced the *dabka*. They learned how to plough the soil and tend a flock and how to be brave and daring. They learned all of this from the Arabs, living *like* them, *near* them, but not *with* them. The Jew who learned to pick stones and oranges later competed with the more experienced and less expensive Arab worker for the same job; the Jew who learnt how to be a farmer later settled on land bought from rich *effendis* living in the city and drove off the *fellaHiin* who had tilled that soil before him. The Jew wearing a *kufiyya* looked at his Arab neighbour, then looked at himself in the mirror and saw both himself and the Other with the romantic eyes of the past (Nir, 1985). The Arab resembled Abraham and other biblical ancestors. The Jew was Isaac, the son of Abraham, back to fulfill the biblical promise and inherit the land. The fact that the Arab was the other son, Ismael, was overlooked by most Jews. Some scholars such as Yitzhak Ben Zvi and writers like Rabbi Binyamin even claimed that Palestinian Arabs were the descendants of the ancient Jews and should be invited back to Judaism.

The Hebrew language, dormant for centuries and mainly used for religious practice and research, was now revived as an important facet of national revival. The leader of this revival, Eliezer Ben Yehuda, a Jerusalem journalist of Russian origin, coined many new words and terms in the newspapers he edited, and compiled the first historical dictionary of the Hebrew language. In the preface to his dictionary (1940/1960: 10) he wrote:

> I particularly compared the roots of our language with those of Arabic [. . .] since this consistent similarity makes the reader realize how close these two languages are in nature and spirit, so much so that they are almost **one and the same**. It is this realization that explains and justifies my constant practice of borrowing handfuls of Arabic in order to fill the voids in our language wherever its vocabulary lacks some root from which the necessary word may smoothly be coined. (Emphasis in the original)

Translation fitted into this picture of intercultural contact in four different ways, including three cases in which Jews were involved and one involving Israeli Arabs.

Noblemen and Heroes: The Arab as a Model for the Jew

The first case where literary translation from Arabic into Hebrew served as a tool in the attempt to close the intercultural gap between the Jewish and Arab communities took place towards the end of the Ottoman rule of Palestine.

The first translations from Arabic into Hebrew were made by a group of Jewish scholars who lived in Jerusalem and belonged to the small aristocratic community of well-to-do Oriental Jews who had lived in Palestine prior to the first Zionist immigration. To these people the Arab was neither the noble savage nor the threatening Gentile that he later became to the European newcomers. He was the neighbour they grew up with, and his language was one they could speak and read. The Hebrew University was inaugurated in 1925 and its Institute of Oriental Studies opened in 1926. Before that Arabic could not be studied at an academic level in Palestine so some of those Jews went to Germany to read for their doctorates in Arabic. To get first-hand knowledge of Arabic language and culture they also took private lessons with Arab scholars and sheiks and learned the Holy *Qur'an* and *Hadith*. They lived with Arabs in Jerusalem and tried to persuade their Jewish brothers to become more familiar with Arab culture, believing that the only chance for the Jews to integrate into the Middle East was through cooperation with the Arabs. They translated the academic texts they had studied, including pre-Islamic poetry and Hadith, as well as ancient and contemporary folktales and proverbs. One of them, Yoel Yoseph Rivlin, later translated *The Holy Quran* and *The Arabian Nights*. At the end of the 19th century the Jewish community in Palestine was extremely small and most of its cultural activity, through publication of newspapers and magazines, was concerned with descriptions of the new Jewish settlements in Palestine. The group under discussion fortunately found the magazine *Luah Eretz Yisrael* (The Palestinian Calendar) (1896–1916) that welcomed them and regularly published their translations from Arabic. The other materials it published were of two kinds:

(1) Current news and stories about Jewish settlements and historical and archaeological data about Jewish people in their ancient homeland. In this it resembled other Jewish publications.
(2) Articles describing Arab ways of life, including both Beduines and *fel-laHin*. For the editor Avraham Noshe Lunz, an expert on ancient Jewish history in Palestine, publishing translations in ancient Arabic prose and poetry served a double purpose: Firstly, to make Jewish readers respect the Arabs for their rich heritage and its values and to point out the possibility of Jewish-Arab coexistence which prevailed in ancient times, namely the *Jahiliyya* and the golden age in medieval Spain; and secondly to contribute to the creation of a new and better Jew through the inspiration of the social and moral values depicted in those transla- tions. Translators' introductions to the translated texts connected them not only with the historical periods during which Jews and Arabs had lived and worked together but also with biblical times, adopting the romantic Zionist view of the contemporary Arab as reminiscent of ancestral biblical figures. The texts chosen for translation praised such social values as valour, courage and generosity. The Arab, then, again served as both model and mirror, this time also seen in his own right.

A quotation from Avraham Shalom Yahudah's introduction to his short collection of translations *Arab Noblemen and Heroes* (1896: 89–90) may illus- trate the latter point:

> The Hebrew reader may enjoy learning about the ways of the Arab people, their manners and habits since they became a nation upon the earth 2300 years ago, for they were very much like our own ancestors at the time when they still peacefully lived upon their land. Both were similar in conduct, generosity, feeding the hungry and faithfully pro- tecting their neighbours and those who sought shelter under their roofs. Hebrew readers may be even happier to learn that many of our

brothers, the Children of Israel, lived peacefully among the Arabs during that period and they were no lesser than the latter. For they, too, begot great leaders such as Adiyyah and Shmuel his son who devoted their lives to better their neighbours' lives and those of the people with whom they dwelt and from among them, too, some heroes emerged. They too, became famous in Arab history for their heroic feats, fidelity, bravery and poetry.

Yahudah further draws a picture of the _Jahiliyya_ as a mutual Jewish-Arab golden age by referring to the only known Jewish poet of the time as-Samau'al b. Adiyyah. This poet, of whose work only fragments have survived, became famous for keeping his faith to prince and poet Imru'u al-Qais who had entrusted him with his precious family weapons. as-Samau'al refused to give them up to his friend's enemy, although the latter killed one of his sons. The proverb _a'wfaa min as-Samau'al_ (more faithful than as-Samau'al), that depicts him as the epitome of faithfulness refers to this story, and his poem, the _laamiyya_, translated by Yahudah in his afore-mentioned collection, remains popular to this day. However, beside the Hebrew names of as-Samau'al and his father there is nothing particularly Jewish about either the poem or the story behind it, which depicts a proud _Jahiliyyi Sayyid_, the leader of his people.

An Arab Mask in the Mirror of Israeli Hebrew Literature

Whereas translations of ancient Arabic literature into Hebrew helped fill some cultural gaps in the emerging new Jewish identity in Palestine and were exercised by a homogeneous cultural group of translators, pseudo-translations of modern Arabic literature served only a small number of individual writers at a later stage, when Israeli Jewish culture and literature had already created their own independent models.

These cases were an exception to a rule, as throughout the period under discussion Israeli Hebrew literature abounded with descriptions of Arabs, most of which were extremely stereotypical (Domb, 1982; Ramraus-Rauch, 1989), sometimes even metaphorical (Perry, 1986). Only rarely were Arabs described as fully fledged literary figures with real conflicts and emotions. Arab stereotypes included the depiction of the Arab as enemy, violent and dumb. An outstanding example is the old Arab whose tongue was cut off in A.B. Yeshosua's novella _Facing the Forest_ (1963). It describes a Jewish student sent out to guard a forest planted on the ruins of an Arab village. The student sets fire to the forest and consequently traces of the Arab past are revealed. Yeshosua's old Arab has been interpreted by Jewish literary critics and researchers as representing the Israeli Arab who lost his voice in the state of Israel (Laor, 1995). According to another stereotype Arab men and women were described as physically attractive to Jews, an attraction often mixed with aggression. A prominent example are the Arab twins Halil and Aziz, the childhood playmates of Hannah, the heroine of Amos Oz's novel *My Dear Michael* (1968), who return to rape her in her dreams. Even romantic love affairs were doomed to fail in Israeli Hebrew literature since mixed marriages with Arab partners are generally not permitted in . Israeli reality.

Against this background it is interesting to study those few cases where Israeli Hebrew writers hid behind a borrowed Arab persona and produced pseudo-translations, pretending to be non-existent Arab writers and publishing their original Hebrew literary works as if these were translations from the Arabic.

Cases of pseudo-translation are well-known in other instances of intercultural contact (Toury, 1995: 40–52) where the claimed source culture is usually considered as superior to the presumed target culture, so that it is worth presenting one's own work as coming from a more prestigious source. In the case of Arabic and Hebrew, however, Arabic culture is generally considered by Hebrew culture as either non-existent or inferior, so there was no obvious gain to be made from pretending to have borrowed from it. What, then, made Israeli Jewish writers hide behind an invented Arab identity in spite of these unfavourable circumstances? The two cases described here provide two different answers to this question.

In the first case, Yisrael Eliraz, a playwright noted for the opera libretti he writes to the music of Israeli composer Joseph Tal, invented an Arab persona by the name of Georges Matiyya Ibrahim, a Palestinian born in Bethlehem and studying and living in Paris. Ibrahim presumably wrote poems in French, in which he expressed his longing for his home town and the beautiful landscapes of the West Bank, and sent them to Eliraz, with whom he had studied in Paris, who translated them into Hebrew. The pseudo-translations were produced and published over a long period (1979–1987) during which Eliraz also published a volume of poetry in his own name, the similarity of which to the presumably 'translated' poems aroused no suspicion. They were applauded for their beauty and elaborate style and published in several prominent literary magazines as well as two collections (1980/1988; 1984). When Eliraz finally admitted the truth he was interviewed by both the Hebrew and Arabic press about his reasons for the pretence. He explained that he had long been known as playwright and librettist, so when he attempted to write poetry he did not want to be judged by his past achievements. Therefore he chose to hide behind a persona with which he shared many biographical details – Georges Matiyya Ibrahim was a real Palestinian student he had known in Paris. Eliraz's explanation provides an excuse for hiding behind a persona but does not explain his choice of an Arab one. I suggest that Eliraz who, like many Israeli Jewish writers, politically identifies with left-wing ideology, chose Ibrahim as his alter ego to be able to express his own love for the sights and landscapes he had known as a child in pre-1948 Palestine and was now happy to see again. Since this was only made possible after the Israeli occupation of the West Bank in 1967, to which Eliraz personally objected, he chose to hide behind a West Bank Arab living away from his home town and to borrow his legitimate longing.

In the second case, prose writer Yoram Kaniuk wrote about such painful aspects of Israeli Jewish identity as the psychological state of Holocaust survivors and the despair of badly wounded war veterans who faced loss of physical beauty. When it came to describing an Arab's inner conflict, however, Kaniuk chose to hide behind an Arab persona and write a novel *A Good Arab* . . . (1984) under the pseudonym Yusuf Shararah. The three dots at the end of the Hebrew hint at a particularly ugly cliché used by some Israeli Jews – 'A good Arab is a dead one'.

The novel is presumably autobiographic. It depicts the hopeless situation faced by the son of a mixed marriage between an Arab man and a Jewish woman who can find no foothold in either society. Unlike the mask worn by Eliraz that was kept intact for four years, Kaniuk's pretence was found out within months by Anton Shammas, an Israeli bilingual poet and translator who easily recognised the writer's unique Hebrew style. Kaniuk, who had often participated in political demonstrations against injustice done to Arabs in both Israel and the occupied territories, chose to hide behind Yusuf Shararah's persona in order to describe the same injustice through literary means. Since his act cannot be attributed to fear of openly expressing his opinion it may be because of his wish to write in the first person singular so as to make the story sound more direct and authentic.

In the two categories described so far literary translations from Arabic into Hebrew were used to enrich the Israeli Jewish cultural identity. The next two categories describe cases where similar translations were used to preserve the translators' Arab cultural identity.

'Arabic was my First Language:' Preserving Iraqi Jewish Identity

The establishment of the state of Israel was followed by mass Jewish immigration from the Arab countries. Absorption into Israeli society at that time meant having to fit into the model of 'The New Israeli'. All immigrant Jews were expected to become Hebrew speakers who would quickly adapt to the local codes of social behaviour and sever their old ties with other cultures and languages. Consequently, immigrants from the Arab countries had to give up the Arab part of their identity to become part of the Israeli sociocultural 'melting-pot'.

Although most Arab immigrants complied, some of them made a different choice. These were young educated Iraqi Jews who were in their late teens or early twenties but who had already started careers as university students, practising journalists or poets. They were members of the Iraqi Communist Party and came to Israel not out of a passion for Zionism but to escape hanging for their political activities. Though young, they already had a clear cultural identity that they refused to give up. They filled various official positions in the young state of Israel which needed people with a good command of Arabic but did not trust its Arab citizens. These positions included work in the official Arab press and radio, supervising the Israeli Arab educational system and running the Arab affairs departments created within governmental bodies, political parties and the *Histadrut*, the official trade union. Some of the Iraqi Jewish immigrants studied Arabic at Israeli universities as well as abroad and became lecturers in modern Arabic literature in Israeli universities. A prominent member of this group, Sasson Somekh, born in Baghdad, had been a teenage poet whose talent was recognised by Al-Jawahiri, Iraq's great revolutionary poet, and had been close to the poets of the *Shi'r* innovative school. As soon as he immigrated to Israel he studied Hebrew with the intention of translating Arabic literature into it. As professor of modern Arabic literature at Tel Aviv University, he became famous for his study of Naguib Mahfouz (1973). Somekh has translated and published hundreds of poems and a number of short stories and supervised translation projects for which he enlisted his students and colleagues as translators. A case in point is the translation of the trilogy of Naguib Mahfouz (1981, 1984, 1987) by Sami Michael, another Baghdad-born Jewish immigrant who made his name as a Hebrew writer.

Somekh further promoted translations from Arabic into Hebrew by publishing collections of poetry translated both by himself and by others, including an anthology of Syrian and Lebanese poets of the *shi'r* school (1973) and collections of Israeli Arabic poetry by Michel Haddad (1979) and Siham Daud (1981), whose style is reminiscent of the *shi'r* school. In both of these projects, Somekh continued to nurture the poetry he had known and loved in Iraq.

Somekh was further involved in publishing translations and supervising translation projects in various Israeli literary supplements and magazines. He particularly contributed to the monthly *Iton77* (The 1977 Magazine) in which he served as special adviser for translations from Arabic. Since the 1970s, when Israelis took a growing interest in Egyptian and Palestinian literatures because of changes in political circumstances, most of the Israeli press has welcomed translations from Arabic literature. *Iton77* has gone even further: it has regularly published translations from Arabic as part of its overt literary policy. Most of the 265 issues published so far have included translations of Arabic poetry and prose, while several special issues have been dedicated to translations from Arabic literature, with particular emphasis on Palestinian literature.

A major contribution to translations from Arabic made by another scholar of Iraqi Jewish origin was the first anthology of Palestinian literature prepared by Shimon Ballas (1970), a Hebrew writer and professor of modern Arabic literature at Haifa University. Ballas had written a PhD at the Sorbonne on the subject of 'Arabic Literature under the Shadow of War' that dealt with the Palestinian plight. His anthology included some of the Palestinian short stories he had studied in which the Arab refugees' suffering and anguish were depicted.

Whereas Somekh, Ballas and other scholars of Iraqi-Jewish origin became translators as soon as they mastered Hebrew, other Iraqi Jews joined the translator ranks much later, some 30 and even 40 years after their immigration to Israel. This late blooming may be attributed to their belated wish to reconcile the Arab side of their identity, which they had repressed so long so as to become absorbed in Israel via their Israeli Jewish side of which they now felt reassured. A prominent case is that of Hebrew writer Sami Michael who wrote several novels about his childhood and youth in Baghdad, the suffering of Oriental Jews after emigrating to Israel and good Jewish-Arab relations in Haifa. Michael wrote the following about the way he used his translation of the *Trilogy* by Mahfouz to reconcile his Arab side with the Hebrew one:

Arabic was my first language and my only knowledge of Hebrew was through a few words that seeped into my consciousness through my father's and grandfather's prayers. When I switched into Hebrew I activated a strict repression apparatus with regard to Arabic, which I stopped reading and writing. I kept as far as possible from the No Man's Land that lies between these two languages in order to have a better command of Hebrew which I studied on my own, neither at school nor at the university. Translating the great work by Mahfuz made me return to the intervening area that lies between these two languages. I had lived in the No Man's Land between these two languages, between the two cultures and the two identities, the Hebrew one and the Arabic one. Life in this part of the world requires a considerable amount of forgetting in order to be able to forgive. (Michael, 1993: 9–10)

Writing with Both Hands: Israeli Arab Writers as Translators of Arabic Literature into Hebrew

Translation of Arabic literature into Hebrew has also played a significant role in shaping the identity of Israeli Arabs who tried to reconcile their Arab nationality with their Israeli citizenship. These translators worked on an individual basis but shared some common cultural traits – they all belonged to the first generation of Arabs educated in the state of Israel who studied Arabic as their first language and Hebrew as their second one from elementary school onward. Their university education was mainly in Hebrew, the predominant language in Israeli universities used for teaching even in most Arabic language and literature departments.

The national disaster that befell the Arabs of Palestine in 1948 involved the loss of most of their cultural and literary elite. The new generation of Arab scholars and writers nurtured by the few remaining poets and educators was born in the early 1950s and reached maturity in the early 1970s. By this time the Israeli government had revoked the military government imposed on Israeli Arabs (1948–1968), and access to higher education and direct contact with Jews and Hebrew culture became easier. The 1967 war made some Israelis realise that the Palestinians who had vanished in 1948 were back to stay. As a result, Israeli literature, drama and cinema began to take a growing interest in the Palestinian plight and voices calling for a peaceful solution of the Israeli-Arab conflict began to be heard. This changing atmosphere was reflected by literary translations in both directions, Arabic-Hebrew and Hebrew-Arabic, sponsored by Israeli official and voluntary bodies working towards Jewish-Arab mutual understanding. Several young Israeli Arabs who already occupied prominent positions in Israeli Arabic culture as poets and editors of literary magazines now sought to occupy similar ones in the dominant Hebrew culture, without deserting their Arab heritage and found translation a perfect way to combine the two.

The most successful Arab translator into Hebrew has been Anton Shammas. Born in the village of Fasuta in the Upper Galilee he later took a BA in English literature and the History of Art at the Hebrew University in Jerusalem. He was the secretary of the Arabic literary magazine *sh-sharq* and translated Hebrew literature into Arabic; subsequently he wrote in the Hebrew press, translated literature in both directions and became an extremely popular journalist in both languages. In 1974 he was asked to edit a bilingual anthology, *bi sawt muzdawij* (twin voices) for *bayt al-karma* (The House of the Vine), a Jewish-Arab community centre in Haifa, the only one of its kind in Israel. The anthology was prepared specially for an encounter between Israeli Jewish and Arab writers and the works were chosen by the participants. As a result of the success of this encounter two more such encounters and anthologies followed in 1975 and 1976. The anthologies were not for sale and their distribution was limited to the participants in the encounters. Yet they were a historical breakthrough – they were the first anthologies devoted to texts written by Israeli Arabs and edited by an Arab and some of their texts were recycled in magazines and other anthologies. Shammas later became famous as the translator of Emile Habiby's three novels: *al-mutash'il* (*The Pessoptimist*), *ekhtayya* and *saraaya bint al-ghuul*. Habiby's bitter criticism of both Israeli Jews and Arabs expressed in those novels was welcomed by Israeli Hebrew culture, thanks to Shammas' brilliant translations and his intricate Hebrew style. The Palestinian plight depicted by Habiby was often referred to by Israeli critics as reminiscent of the suffering of the Jews in the diaspora. As in the cases discussed earlier, the Israeli Jew looked at the Arab and saw a reflection of himself.

The growing recognition of Habiby's position as a prominent writer was reflected by change of publishing houses – *The Pessoptimist* was published by Mifras, a small private radical publishing house concerned with social and political injustice, which regularly published translations of Arabic novels, with special emphasis on Palestinian literature. *ekhtayya* was published by the mainstream publishing house Am Oved in its small-scale non-commercial series devoted to literary works that depict social injustice. *saraaya* was published by Siman Kriah Books which publishes prestigious works with a high sales potential. Shammas' translation of *The Pessoptimist* was also adapted for stage by the popular theatre and cinema actor Muhammad Bakri who later performed two parallel versions of the play – an Arabic one and a Hebrew one (1986–1995). Habiby's unprecedented success in Hebrew translation was thus promoted by two Israeli Arab catalysts, Shammas and Bakri. It culminated in his receiving the prestigious Israel Prize for literature in 1994, never before or after awarded to an Arab.

Another translator was Muhammad Hamza Ghanaim who was born in the village of Baqa al-Gharbiyyah in the Israeli Triangle area. Like Shammas he, too, started out as a poet and editor in Arabic then became a translator both from Hebrew into Arabic and Arabic into Hebrew. Between 1984 and 1988 he was editor of the bilingual magazine *Liqaa'-Mifgash* (*Encounter*). Just as the anthologies edited by Shammas were sponsored by the Ministry of Education, the Haifa municipality and other official bodies, *Liqaa'* was sponsored by the Histradrut Trade Union which did not interfere with the editor's literary and ideological policy. This project was more ambitious than the previous one – the texts it published included prose, poetry and articles, many of which discussed the cultural Jewish-

Arab encounter, which was presented by Israeli Arab and Jewish writers as highly desirable. The literature published consisted of up-to-date works by both Israeli writers and poets and those from various parts of the Arab world. Ghanaim wished to introduce both Israeli Jews and Arabs to one another and to the Arab world respectively, in an attempt to reconcile all three. This project was partially successful – the magazine was welcomed by the Israeli Jewish press thanks to its high literary and artistic quality, while those few Arab critics who responded to it at all bitterly criticised Ghanaim for taking the Israeli side and ignored his attempt at treble cultural reconciliation.

Conclusion

The cases described demonstrate the role played by translations of Arabic literature into Hebrew as a feature of Israeli Jews' and Arabs' quest for identity at a time of constant political and armed conflict. The future may hopefully bring new models of Jewish-Arab cultural encounter created in an atmosphere of peace.

Chapter 6

Translating Islamist Discourse

MIKE HOLT

Islamist discourse is becoming increasingly important in political and cultural life in the Arab world. Both oppositions and ruling regimes often articulate and legitimise their positions through Islam. But the translation of this discourse is, I believe, of particular interest, not only because of its prevalence and importance, but because of the particular problems it poses theoretically and practically.

Firstly, it is a discourse that attempts to speak from outside the orbit of the West and to challenge notions of universality based on European models, yet few in the West are aware of the basic tenets of this ideology. Some writers, such as Sayyid Qutb, whom I will refer to in this chapter, have been hugely influential in the Arab world but are rarely read by Western readers. More often than not, they read second-hand accounts filtered and digested for them by Western based academics, always open to the charge of orientalism. So, all the more reason for Islamists to be heard directly or as directly as translation allows and all the more reason why the translators' art must be closely scrutinised. We need to see if a text expressly antithetical to another culture can be translated into the language of that 'Other'.

Secondly, these texts bring with them specific problems for the translator, especially concerning intertextuality, rhetorical devices unfamiliar to most English speaking readers and, above all, the connotive and affective aspects of Islamic terminology so consistently used by Islamist writers to persuade their Arabic readership of the truth, moral justification and even inevitability of their arguments. It will be edifying to see how or even if the translators attempt to overcome these problems and with what degree of success.

So what is meant by Islamism and therefore by the discourse associated with it? Briefly, Islamism is first and foremost a political ideology and more specifically one that articulates its analysis of power and its political plan of action through the religious terms and concepts found in Islam. Although

63

the term 'Muslim fundamentalism' is often used in the West it is deliberately avoided here for two reasons: firstly, fundamentalism is a term borrowed from a description of radical Christian groups in America, then extended to other religions on the grounds of superficial similarities. Clearly, describing political movements in the Muslim world in terms coined for Christian groups in the West runs into all kinds of problems. Secondly, the term fundamentalism refers to a belief in the literal truth of the Bible, which liberals in the West see as unorthodox, the preferred contemporary view being to see much of the Bible as allegory or metaphor. A belief in the literal truth of the Qur'an is the mainstream view in Islam and is not what distinguishes Islamist activists from the general population: accordingly the term is inappropriate.

Working from the premise that Islamism is basically political discourse, what are its main features? By referring to 'main features', I conclude that all the different Islamist ideologues and groups share something in common. It is as acceptable to talk in general about Islamism as it is to talk about Marxism or Liberalism and that there are features common to most Islamist discourse, although groups may differ widely in their interpretation of this discourse, style of leadership, etc.

Perhaps rather than simply listing a set of core concepts it would be more instructive to trace the reasons for the emergence of Islam in the latter half of the twentieth century as the main challenge to ruling regimes in much of the Muslim world. How is it that states as diverse as Afghanistan, Algeria, Egypt, Sudan, Turkey and even Trinidad and Tobago should witness either a direct threat to their power or indeed be overthrown by Islamist groups? For a global explanation, rather than a specific one, I have drawn on the work of Bobby Sayyid (1997), not only because he provides an elegant and convincing argument but also because his thesis is linked to linguistic theory and to modernity. In short, Sayyid sees the emergence of Islamism as a direct result of what is called the 'decentring of the West' where the West is no longer the uncontested model of human progress and development and the history of the West cannot be seen as an unchallenged record of that progress. The reasons for this fall from grace are described by a number of authors, many working within a post-modern critique. Some reasons are internal to the West, such as the two world wars, the Holocaust, ecological disaster and theoretical advocacy of a pluralist and diverse culture which all question the idea of unilinear progress and universality. The clearest example of an external factor would be decolonisation, where political separation usually invokes ideological distancing although, of course, new independent regimes often come to resemble those they replaced. Interestingly, Robert Young (1990) traces the origins of post-modern thought to the Arab world itself, to the aftermath of the Algerian war of independence and to French writers such as Sartre, Derrida and Lyotard who had been affected by the war, and often themselves had strong personal links with Algeria.

But perhaps the most salient point in Sayyid's analysis of post-modernism stems from the argument that post-modernism disentangles the West from modernism. Others have tried to argue that a rejection of the West is a rejection of modernism but Sayyid holds that the two are no longer coterminous. Islamism, then, in very general terms, is a rejection of Western or European political models, but not of modernism or progress. Khomeini and Qutb are not anti-modern, or indeed anti-science or anti-progress. Hence another reason for the inappropriacy of fundamentalism, which suggests a return, a going-back. They are simply anti- or even non-Western since this is from where much of the popularity of Islam is derived.

Modern regimes in the Muslim world, which Sayyid calls Kemalist regimes, have been discredited and along with them their borrowed Western ideologies. What is required to challenge these regimes is another type of discourse capable of becoming hegemonic; in other words a discourse able to describe all other discourses in its terms and dominate them. Islamist discourse, borrowing as it does so much from Islam itself, has been readily available to take over from failed Western ideologies to offer hope and a political plan of action, untainted by charges of being in the service of Western states or alien to ordinary Muslims' way of life.

The linguistic part of Sayyid's account stems from a Saussurean discussion of the relationship between signifier and signified. Signifiers normally refer to more than one signified, the phenomenon of polysemy. In temporal terms they 'tend to preserve traces of previous articulations' and these traces are organised in chains by the mechanisms of metaphor and metonymy (Sayyid, 1997: 42). Nowhere is this more true than in Islam where terms like *Hijra* or *Jihad* carry layer upon layer of connotive meaning. But what is to stop signification multiplying into meaninglessness or vague abstraction, given that no signifier has one signified? The potential for 'slippage' is held back or tied into place by nodal points in the structure of a given discourse. These knots of meaning help to stabilise the other elements around them. Islam, then, would be a nodal point in a number of discourses such as *Fiqh* or everyday Muslim worship. Moreover, in a given community one signifier often comes to symbolise and structure all other discourses because it becomes the concept by which that community is defined. It no longer refers to any one thing because it is too large and operates in so many different discourses and therefore becomes a *master signifier*, which, in Sayyid's words, 'functions as a metonymy for the whole discursive universe' (1997: 45). So the Islamist project is to make Islam the master signifier for all discourses including the political, the cultural and the social, whereas the regimes it opposes would either prefer Islam to be confined to discourses unconnected with political power or else claim they represent true Islam and the Islamists merely a distortion. Even in the latter case, secular regimes are, perhaps unwittingly, being pushed into a corner where political discourse still becomes dominated by the master signifier of Islam, and where they may be less adept at justifying their existence with relation to Islam than their Islamist opponents.

Islam, as a master signifier for Muslim communities, comes to unify and to represent what may otherwise appear fragmented and perplexing and at the same time to symbolise what Sayyid calls 'Goodness incarnate' (1997: 48). Hence the Islamist claim that the best government is Islamic government amounts to saying the best government is good government, which is hard to refute unless you try to break the link either between Islam and good or between Islamists and true Islam. The limits of the master signifier, however, have to be set, and with large signifiers such as 'Islam' or 'Nation' it is often through the attendant notion of 'evil incarnate' which, in the case of a particular nation, may be another historical enemy nation or, in the case of Islam, as articulated by Islamicists, it is *jahiliyya* society or the West.

The general significance from a discourse perspective of this view of Islamism is as follows: it is a form of political discourse, but one which challenges the status quo, both locally and globally, by proposing Islam as a master signifier for all discourses and where Islam symbolises the greatest good and defines the community, rather than the state, language or tribe. Moreover, it is also defined negatively as antipathetic to the West, to secularism and to local rule.

This is, of course, the source of the difficulties any translator will have to overcome when translating these texts into English. How does one successfully translate a master signifier into another frame of reference where it neither identifies a community nor ties together other discursive universes? And how does the translator convey the chains of articulation of terms with over 1400 years of history? Is it possible to communicate to the antagonistic Other whose existence is essential to set the boundaries for the new *Umma*?

To examine these issues I have chosen *Ma'aalim fi T-Tariiq* by Sayyid Qutb (1981) translated into English by American Trust Publications as *Milestones* (Qutb, 1990). The actual translator(s) remain anonymous as no names or other information appear in the English version. Despite the original being widely read in Islamist circles, it is not easily obtainable in translation and yet is cited in almost every general book in English on the subject of Islamism.

Space does not allow anything but the briefest of relevant details of Qutb and his work. The Egyptian Sayyid Qutb (1906–1966) is regarded by many as the leading Islamist ideologue of the twentieth century. He became a fierce critic of Nasser and his brand of Islamic Socialism and was imprisoned for his pains. This book first appeared in 1964, two years before Qutb was hanged for treason. It marks a complete break from the reformist tradition of Muhammad Abdu and his attempted synthesis of Islam with Western principles. Qutb attempts no such synthesis – his message is articulated in purely indigenous terms with no textual references to Western sources, although he shows familiarity with Marxism and Capitalism in the opening chapter. In a chapter on what I would call Nationalism vs. Theocracy and entitled in Arabic *jinsiyyatu l-muslimi 'aqiidatuh* there is not one single reference, bibliographic or otherwise, to Europe or to Western sources, despite the fact that this is where nationalism and the nation state started. He does not refer to the French Revolution, or indeed to Egyptian nationalism under Nasser, although this may be due to considerations of self-preservation. Considering Qutb himself lived in the West for two years and considering his obvious erudition this must be interpreted as a conscious choice rather than a genuine lack of familiarity with Western concepts. Qutb chose to use only Arabic and Islamic sources because he wanted to argue for a purely Islamic model, where Islam would be the master signifier for political discourse and where no concessions were to be made to Western concepts or ideology. Indeed in the second chapter, 'The Unique Qur'anic Generation', he states that what separated the first generation of Muslims from the rest was 'the loss of purity of the first source of Islamic guidance that was mixed with various alien sources' (1990: 13). He goes on to argue, in a theme which reoccurs in Islamist discourse, that the present generation also needs to cut itself off from all alien sources and drink solely from the original spring. But this call for a return to original sources is not traditionalism or conservatism. It is clear that Qutb is rearticulating these themes for future action – future action aimed at taking power both in Egypt and eventually throughout the Muslim world. It is also part of the process of decentring the West through a discourse centred in the East and Islam. So the chapter on nationalism is not pretending that the West does not exist; indeed Qutb acknowledges Western progress in the opening chapter. He prefers rather to root the whole debate in terms related to Muslim theology and history. Hence references to the multi-ethnicity of companions of the Prophet (Bilal, Suhaib, Salman) and to the fact that Islam does not distinguish between believers on the basis of race or nationality, rather than discussing the wars and suffering which resulted from European nationalism. But this rearticulation, of course, refers to something different from the original Qur'anic quotations and *Hadith*, while at the same time retaining strongly visible traces of the original signification. Qutb is now referring to Islam in a world of nation states, to the division of the Muslim world into separate and often antagonistic regimes, to the abolition of the Caliphate and to the competing demands made on the loyalty of his compatriots to the Egyptian state and Nasser rather than to Islam.

Before moving on to a comparison of the two texts, the final general point about *Milestones* I would like to discuss is its intended readership. Qutb makes it clear that he is interested in praxis, not abstract theorising. If Muslim society is to regain world leadership then it must take 'a concrete form in a society, or more precisely in a nation' (1990: 7). This will be brought about by a vanguard that will establish true Islam, which will then spread through nominally Muslim societies which have lost their way. In the opening chapter he writes, 'I have written Milestones for this vanguard, which I consider a uniting reality about to be realized' (1990: 9). In many ways this has proved to be the case. *Milestones* has been most popular amongst Islamist activists who have responded directly to Qutb's call for action. In fact it is probably because of its appeal, mainly amongst these activists, that *Milestones* became widely read only in the late 1970s and 1980s, when the political climate in the Arab and Muslim world had changed and when secular and nationalist solutions had become unpopular and the process of decentring of the West was in full flight. So another question one can ask of the English translation is whether it will be readily understood by an English speaking Muslim vanguard or by a wider readership.

If one skims through the English version at speed one of the first observations is that the translation has retained a great deal of *Arabicness*. Most pages contain at least one of the following four types of direct reference to Arabic, arranged in what I consider to be ascending order of unfamiliarity by a target readership:

(1) Words of Arabic origin now assimilated into English and found in most dictionaries. This list, as one would expect, includes the master signifier *Islam*, words such as *Muslim, Allah*, the *Qur'an*, etc. Clearly the translation of these terms is generally unproblematic from a semantic aspect and it is difficult to suggest an alternative. However, the fact that they retain phonetic features of the original, or are phonemic translations as Lefevre would say, does not mean they carry the same force in English or carry the same chains of articulation.

(2) Quotations from the Qur'an and *Hadith* translated into English. Qur'anic quotations are sometimes indicated with a footnote together with the number of the relevant *sura* and verse at the foot of the page. Here the relationship between the Arabic source text and the English target text is not as clear cut. For example, in the following passage

from the English version, there are Qur'anic quotations without references, which are included in the Arabic original:

> And remember the time when your sustainer said to the angels, 'I will create a viceregent on earth'. I have only created jinns and men that they may serve me. (Qutb, 1990: 6)

Compare this with the Arabic version:

> idh qaala rabbuka lilmala'ika innii jaa'ilun fi l-arDi khaliifa (al-Baqara: 30).
> wa ma khalaqtu l-jinna wal-insa illa liya'buduun (ath-Thaariyyaat: 56).

As the English examples are immediately followed by further Qur'anic quotations, which are given references, the English reader can assume only that the sole direct quotation is: 'I will create a viceregent on earth.'

(3) Arabic quotations reproduced in italicised transliteration with a gloss in English in the first instance but not usually thereafter. For example, *Al-Amin aS-Saadiq* (the trustworthy and truthful) *La ilaha illa Allah* (There is no God except Allah). For an Arabist or a Muslim this normally presents no problem since, when the quotation is subsequently repeated in transliteration but without gloss, it is well-known and accessible. However, to a reader familiar with neither Arabic nor with Islam it would be difficult to remember the original gloss on every occasion. In the absence of a glossary the only recourse would be to search back through the text until the first instance appeared with a gloss.

(4) Arabic words and concepts transliterated but not translated. This includes key concepts such as *jahiliyya* and *din*. The first instance of the use of *jahiliyya* in the English version is in the following sentence:

> If we look at the sources and foundations of modern modes of living, it becomes clear that the whole world is steeped in Jahiliyya and all the marvellous material comforts and advanced inventions do not diminish its ignorance! (Qutb, 1990: 8)

It would be hard for a non-expert to conclude from this that *jahilliyya* and ignorance refer to the same thing. Of course the word *jahiliyya* is in the original Arabic text. But in the next example the word *din* is neither translated nor in the original: 'this concept and the way of life covering all the practical aspects of man's life is the vital message that mankind lacks. We call it the Islamic *din*.' Here the word *din* does not even appear in the original. One could comment about other aspects of the translation of this passage but the fact that Arabic has been added to the English version, which was not in the original does seem unusual. Unfortunately an uninformed English reader might also read the word as *din* in English meaning 'noise' – as there is no indication of a long vowel, although the italics should guard against it being interpreted as an authentic English word.

I am not suggesting that all references to the *Arabicness* of the source text are to be avoided. This would result in an extreme form of cultural translation where key Islamic concepts were, for example, translated into Christian terms and where the geographical setting of early Islam would be transposed, say to Britain.

The use of assimilated terms like *Qur'an* and *Islam* and the translation of quotations from the Qur'an do not hinder understanding. After all, although Qutb asserts that there was no Jewish, Christian or Persian influence in the Qur'an, it sounds vaguely familiar (in translation) to anyone who knows, for instance the King James version of the Bible, and this is unsurprising given the shared Semitic and prophetic tradition. But the consistent repetition of transliterated Arabic phrases, mostly without gloss and the use of key concepts such as *jahiliyya* and *din* without translation, suggests an attempt by the translators not only to retain as much Arabic as possible but in some instances to introduce extra Arabic lexis not found in the original. I see this as a deliberate strategy to locate the translation outside Western culture as much as possible. The term *jahiliyya*, for example, is absolutely central to the thesis Qutb propounds – by extending it to those who profess to be Muslim, such as members of the Egyptian state apparatus, he is therefore able to justify violence against those claiming to be fellow Muslims. At the same time it is a rearticulation of a traditional Islamic term with an excellent pedigree. The non-expert English reader will have none of this information and it is hard to see how they could understand it without referring to a commentary on Qutb and his work. Incidentally the only explanatory footnote in the whole translation concerns the word *shirk*, which is explained thus: 'shirk (Arabic) means associating false gods with Allah'. I believe 'polytheism' would be a more accurate translation which could be incorporated into the main text without the need for footnotes. A further example is the sentence:

wa haadha huwa T-Tariiq (1981: 30)

which is translated as:

And this is the way, the *sirat al mustaqim* (1990: 22)

The phrase *siraat al mustaqiim* is obviously well known even to the majority of non-Arab Muslims, as it occurs in the *faatiHa* (The Opening

Chapter of the Qur'an), and it paraphrases and develops the concept of *Tariiq*, the way. Were it to be in the original text it could have been translated as 'the straight path' because this has religious intertextual associations in English. But it is not in the original text and its addition can only perplex the non-expert reader.

We can see the cumulative effect of all this on one page of the English text which is in fact the first page of Chapter Four. It has been quoted at length to show the extent to which the translated text either retains Arabic features or situates itself in non-English discursive patterns.

JIHAD IN THE CAUSE OF ALLAH

The great scholar Ibn Qayyim, in his book *Zad al-Ma'ad*, has a chapter entitled 'The Prophet's treatment of the Unbelievers and the Hypocrites from the beginning of his messengership until his Death.' In this chapter he sums up the nature of Islamic Jihad. The first revelation from Allah that came to the Prophet – peace be on him – was '*Iqra, bismi Rabbika ladhi Khalaq*. (Read, in the name of they [*sic*] Sustainer, Who created.) This was the beginning of his Prophethood. Allah commanded the Prophet – peace be on him – to recite this in his heart. The commandment to preach had not yet come. Then Allah revealed *Ya'ayyuha al-muddathir; qum fa 'anthir* (O you who are enwrapped in your mantle, arise and warn.) Thus, the revelation of '*Iqra*' was his appointment to Prophethood, while *Ya ayyuha al-muddathir* was his appointment to Messengership. Later Allah commanded the Prophet – peace be on him – to warn his near relatives, then his people, then the Arabs who were around them, then all of Arabia, and finally the whole world. Thus for thirteen years after the beginning of his messengership, he called people to Allah through preaching, without fighting or *jizyah*, and was commanded to restrain himself and to practice [*sic*] patience and forbearance.

Then he was commanded to migrate, and later permission was given to fight. Then he was commanded to fight those who fought him, and to restrain himself from those who did not make war against him. Later he was commanded to fight the polytheists until Allah's *din* was fully established. After the command for jihad came, the non-believers were divided into three categories: those with whom the Muslims had peace treaties; the people with whom the Muslims were at war; and the *dhimmies*. (1990: 43)

This passage contains, as one would expect, words of Arabic origin now assimilated into English such as *jihad, Allah, and Islam(ic)*. Although it is neither feasible nor desirable to suggest alternative translations for these terms, as explained above, they do nevertheless introduce an Arabic element, at least at the phonological level, to the English text. Then we find examples of transliterated Arabic complete with English gloss as in *'Iqra'*, *bismi Rabbika* . . . and *Ya 'ayyuha al-Muddathir* . . . Both these Arabic quotations are repeated without gloss later on. It would appear that not only Qutb but also the translators expect the reader to be familiar with the Arabic text of the Qur'an. In addition there are several examples of transliterated Arabic without English gloss such as *Zad al-Ma'ad, jizyah, din* and *dhimmies*, although the last example has an English inflection pattern. Clearly here the non-specialist English language reader would be at a loss to retrieve any meaning from these untranslated terms. The cumulative effect is a sort of hybrid, at times approaching a parallel text.

In some instances it would appear to be a form of code-switching where there is a conscious decision for a speaker to alternate between two codes / languages for a desired communicative effect. Code-switching is usually motivated by a change in topic, for rhetorical effect or to exclude someone familiar with only one of the codes. Deliberate exclusion would appear to be a curious motivation for a translator but another explanation outside of the normal parameters found within the literature on code-switching offers itself. This is connected to Muslim belief about the nature of revelation and the unique qualities of the text of the Qur'an.

The Qur'an is believed to be a fully accurate verbatim record of the message revealed to the Prophet Muhammad by Allah through his intermediary *Jibril*. The sublime literary quality of the surface structure of the message is regarded as part of the proof of its divine origin; how could Muhammad, a clever but illiterate man, have produced such a work without divine intervention? There are also Qur'anic references to Allah's choice of Arabic as the chosen vehicle for a universal message. All this leads to a special status for the original Arabic text. The message was originally in Arabic for a purpose and it is considered the duty of all Muslims, irrespective of nationality or mother tongue, to read the Qur'an in this original form. Translations are used as expedients to aid text exegesis but Muslims from Birmingham to Bombay study the text in classical Arabic. This is the reverse of the Protestant position with regard to the text of the Bible as so clearly articulated by Eugene Nida where the surface form is largely immaterial; what counts is the message. As universal truth can be expressed in any language, the original has no special status. Indeed, as Gentzler observes, 'his translation as exegesis obscures the original text to such a degree that it becomes unavailable to the contemporary reader' (1993: 59). For Muslims, the original text must never be unavailable, cannot be revised and is even considered by some to be untranslatable. How can a human translator presume to know the intention of the text producer when that producer is Allah? Hence those Qur'anic phrases phonemically translated from the Arabic but not interlingually translated are there as part of a

Muslim tradition of leaving quotations from the Qur'an in classical Arabic thus retaining their full historicity.

The motivation, then, for the inclusion of untranslated Qur'anic phrases is not a part of the usual set of motivations for code-switching but the perceived effect for monolingual readers will be the same; unable to process transliterated Arabic when separated from its gloss, they may be able to grasp the elevated status and special reverence shown to Qur'anic text, but they will, nevertheless, be excluded from any understanding of its meaning.

Other instances where single Arabic words not yet assimilated into English are simply transliterated cannot be accommodated within an explanation based on the tradition of Qur'anic quotation. Terms such as *jizyah, jahiliyya, din* and *dhimmmies* are well-known to any Muslim conversant with the basic tenets of the faith and early Muslim history. They could, however, be translated into English without great difficulty but there is a clear decision on the part of the translators to use interlingual translation for words with particular reference to the master signifier Islam. An obvious example is the word *din* which could be rendered as 'religion' without too great a shift or loss. But to use more general terms applicable to other religions threatens to break the link with other nodal points in the overall discourse of Islam. If something has two referents and one of them refers to other things as well then the stability of meaning is harder to maintain. The translators appear to avoid losing both this stability and the specificity associated with Islamic terminology by simply rejecting interlingual translation. Unfortunately, it is precisely the meaning of these specific terms and their place in Qutb's overall conception of the world that is surely of greatest interest to English language readers unable to read the original.

In conclusion, the decentring of the West, initiated in this instance by Qutb, has continued through the work of the English translators. Like the source text, the translation appears to have been written for a vanguard, for a readership already conversant not only with intertextual reference but with the surface forms of Qur'anic Arabic. In fact, in some ways the English translation expects a greater knowledge of Islamic sources than the Arabic, as many of the bibliographic references to the Qur'an and Hadith cited in the original are excluded from the English version, although not in any consistent fashion. This is a case of what Basil Hatim (1997) calls 'manifest intertextuality', at least in the original. In the translation it is nowhere near as manifest and one is often left wondering what the quotation marks are doing in the text when there is no reference to their source. In short, this version cannot be read by a monolingual, monocultural English reader.

These two texts also give the lie to the strong form of the Sapir-Whorf hypothesis that claims that a given natural language inclines its speakers to a particular world-view. Perhaps the translators have cheated in having key words and phrases in transliterated Arabic, but in general I would argue that the English version is as deeply rooted in non-western discursive patterns as the original. In other words the translation is neither successful in conveying an antithetical message in the language of the Other nor does it address the problems of intertextuality and specific rhetorical devices which such texts pose for the translator.

There is a certain logic to a book originally written for Muslim activists in Egypt to be translated for a corresponding readership in English, but it is unfortunate that such an influential work cannot reach a wider audience, particularly given the widespread misconceptions about Islam and the Arab world that are prevalent in the West. For an English translation to reach such a wider audience, a new version would have to be commissioned, one which relies less on transliteration and which makes intertextual references more manifest. This need not result in complete domestication of the Arabic text. Words conveying complex Muslim social beliefs are entering the English language already – words such as *Ramadan, Hijab*, etc., although one could also point to those completely distorted such as *fatwa* and *jihad*. A more professional and sensitive translation could help to introduce further key concepts such as *jahiliyya* and *ummah* into English but only if readers can follow how these signifiers are structured into other discourses and how they relate to the master signifier *Islam*.

Chapter 7

On Translating Oral Style in Palestinian Folktales

IBRAHIM MUHAWI

Introduction

The purpose of this chapter is to explore from a semiotic perspective certain topics in the comparative stylistics of orality and literacy encountered in the process of translating into English the Palestinian folktales included in Muhawi and Kanaana (1989, hereinafter, *M&K*). The ultimate aim is to outline a theory of style that takes into account the cultural semiotics of the genre in the process of translating the folktales.

In 'The Task of the Translator' Walter Benjamin advances the notion of 'translatability', which he bases on his central thesis that translation is a 'mode'. To the extent that translation is a mode, translatability, he says, 'must be an essential feature of certain works' (1969: 70–1). Translation as a mode, which is separate from writing, distinguishes the work of the translator from that of the poet. The task of the translator, Benjamin continues, must 'consist in finding the intended effect . . . upon the language into which he is translating which produces in it the echo of the original' (1969: 76). The word *echo* is most apt when dealing with oral material. In light of this, we see our task as the exploration of the essential features conducive to the translatability of Palestinian Arab folktales by examining the manner in which the intended effect can be achieved in English as an 'echo of the original'. The tales having been orally performed in the Palestinian dialect within the social context of the Arab extended family, rendering them into print in English involved translation not only from one language into another but also from one semiotic system into another – from oral narrative into text.

The Folktale and Oral Narration

Other than the difference in physical manifestation – sound or script – there is a basic difference between the two modes which is anchored in the

75

presence of a living human teller in oral narration. Ong summarises this difference in very general terms by remarking that oral discourse 'looks to pragmatics', or the performance context, while written discourse (what he calls 'chirographic structures') 'looks to syntactics':

> Written discourse develops more elaborate and fixed grammar than oral discourse does because to provide meaning it is more dependent simply upon linguistic structures, since it lacks the normal full existential contexts which surround oral discourse and help determine meaning in oral discourse somewhat independently of grammar. (1982: 37–8)

Without committing ourselves to the basic premise that the oral is less grammatically complex than the written (a view that will not stand the test of, say, Qur'anic revelation or Pre-Islamic Arabic poetry), or the neat bifurcation between 'pragmatics' and 'syntactics' which this formulation seems to espouse, we can still agree that the alteration of the 'existential context' in translation will lead to an inevitable loss in the pragmatic dimension of the discourse. The advantage of a comparative over a straight stylistic analysis is that it obliges us to contextualise the concept of style itself, enabling us to see it as an echo of the culture rather than as a purely linguistic phenomenon having to do only with the decontextualised, formal properties of texts.

Keeping the transformation in the 'existential context' of the discourse in mind and assuming style to be the semiotic indicator par excellence of any linguistic activity, the most pressing questions then become, what constitutes folktale style, what elements of this style are translatable, and how best to convey the living voice of the narrator in writing? Here we can be guided in our inquiry by the theoretical framework underpinning performance theory, which approaches verbal art from the standpoint of sociolinguistics and the ethnography of speaking. Perhaps the most significant aspect of this theory, the aspect that greatly affects the philosophy of translation, is that it grounds performance rhetorically in the audience. Performance is understood to be a culturally defined 'mode of speaking' (Bauman, 1977: 5), or, using our terminology, speaking in a certain style. It is a mode of communication that 'consists in the assumption of responsibility to an audience for a display of communicative competence' (1977: 11). Performance does not necessarily imply theatricality, only an assumption of responsibility. In Palestine it is the women who assume responsibility for a display of communicative competence in narrating folktales; hence, it is their speech that shapes the style of the genre. That women should be the principal narrators of folktales in Palestine is not surprising, given their social role in the structure of the family. They, after all, are responsible for the rearing of children, their entertainment and acculturation. In order to assume responsibility one must also have the competence; the one implies the other. The only successful male tellers, and they are very few, are those who can comfortably adopt some of the mannerisms of women's speech into their narration (e.g. Sha:fi' in *M&K*). Now, if by analogy we see translation as performance, the translator must also possess communicative competence in the target language to assume responsibility, but the audience in this case will be composed of readers rather than listeners. Taking the analogy a little further, and keeping with Benjamin's notion of the echo, we can communicatively describe reading as an act of listening; thus a viable translation should enable readers to hear the folktale in the process of reading, and to read it out loud with pleasure. (For a more extended discussion of translation as performance from a folkoristic perspective, see Muhawi, 2002).

In addressing the question of style, we begin at a most obvious point, a point so transparent that until recently it has been ignored altogether: namely, what kind of discourse is oral narrative composed of? Is it prose, poetry, drama, dramatic poetry? Except for Lüthi (1976, 1982, 1984), most scholars dealing with the Indo-European folk narrative tradition have not concerned themselves much with style. Writing on the European folktale, Lüthi discusses style from a literary perspective, wisely sidestepping the question of discourse type altogether, except for passing references in the middle of other discussion to the folktale as a 'poetic composition' (1982: 112) and 'a short epic form' (1976: 73). Tedlock on the other hand, having studied and translated Zuni oral narratives for many years, concludes that folktales belong to the genre of dramatic oral poetry rather than short-story prose:

> The treatment of oral narrative as dramatic poetry has a number of analytical advantages. Some of the features of oral narrative, which have been branded 'primitive', on the basis of comparisons with written prose fiction, can now be understood as 'poetic' instead. (1983: 51)

Tedlock's solution to the loss of the existential context anchored in the living voice of the teller was to devise a system of translation that uses the alphabet iconically to represent a paralinguistic poetics of performance based on the pause: 'While it may be that past translations of Zuni narratives have suffered somewhat from neglect of the "linguistic" features of style . . . they have suffered much more from neglect of "oral" or "paralinguistic" features such as voice quality (tone of voice), loudness, and pausing' (1983: 45). Certainly, loudness and voice quality are worth noting, Tedlock adds, but pausing is 'foremost among the paralinguistic devices that give shape to Zuni narrative and distinguish it from written prose' (1983: 48).

Tedlock was no doubt motivated to devise his scheme because the presentation of the tellers with whom he worked was highly dramatic, rich in paralinguistic features. Similarly, Seitel indicates that he resorted to Tedlock's method because it is 'the clearest way we have in print to convey some of the theater and poetry of storytelling performances', (1980: vii). But these features are not highlighted in Palestinian oral narration; the older women who tell the tales to the children hardly raise their voices at all, and they certainly do not gesticulate. They let the tale tell itself, relying as much on the context (semi-darkness at evening time) as on the fantastic content and the highly stylised language to do the work. Adult males almost never attend these sessions, and the adult women present would normally be expected to tell at least one tale each. The context and audience here largely define what performance means. The context being intimate and the audience composed of children, the teller's assumption of responsibility for an act of communicative competence consists not in animated delivery but in keeping children entertained by giving the tale its due in terms of language and narrative detail. The children, even before they learn to read, are already fascinated by language. They are conversant with many genres that involve sophisticated use of language, in riddles, jokes, rhymes, ditties and songs of various types. Hence they are a demanding audience. The language must hold their attention. The playful quality we observe in the language is one aspect of this performance that no doubt finds an echo in the children's own folklore and helps to hold their attention. A folktale does not become dramatic just because it is delivered by an animated narrator. If there is drama in the tale it must form part of what Dundes (1980: 22–23) calls 'the texture' of the work, an aspect of its very style. Accordingly, we do not see the folktale as a form of poetic drama; it strikes us that formulation does some violence to the narrative art of the folktale, that dimension of it which contributes most significantly to its translatability because, as has been frequently observed, fiction as a genre of discourse is itself a semiotic system that transcends linguistic categories.

Another important consideration that bears upon folktale translatability has been the ongoing 'contamination' of the genre by textuality and the print medium since at least the fourteenth century in Europe and perhaps even earlier in the Arab tradition. I am not necessarily referring here to the extensive influence of the *Thousand and One Nights* on European literature (cf. Ali, 1981; Caracciolo, 1988; Irwin, 1994), the widespread use of complete folktales or parts thereof in literature, as in Chaucer's *Canterbury Tales*, or their collection after they have been rewritten and modified, as in Bocaccio's *Decameron*. This process has its parallel in Arabic as well, where the *Thousand and One Nights*, itself contaminated by the rhetorical devices used to embellish Arabic poetic prose, has had an immense influence on the

Arabic oral tradition, especially on tellers who have some facility in reading, including Sha:fi'. From a folkloristic perspective, the setting down of the *Nights* in a dialectal Arabic (stylised and embellished to enhance readability) stems from a sound ethnographic impulse to approximate the conditions of performance, except that performance is understood there as falling within the sociolinguistics of register rather than the poetics of paralanguage. All these practices no doubt played an important role in helping to naturalise folk narrative in the print medium, preparing the ground for its translatability; but the contamination I have in mind concerns the 'invention' in the seventeenth century by Charles Perrault and Madame d'Aulnoy of the written fairy tale – a genre that sometimes utilises motifs current in oral tradition – and the subsequent establishment of a European folk narrative canon, especially after the appearance in the middle of the nineteenth century of the Grimm collection. The effect of all this 'contamination' by print has been the creation of the Motif Index and the tale type index, which taken together are the best possible handmaids for the translatability of folktales.

Considered semiotically, genre like style is a sign. Hence when we translate an Arabic folktale into English, we are not only translating an individual performance but an example of a genre that is common to both traditions. Folk narrative style is characterised by frequent resort to different kinds of formulas, and to the extent that oral narrative is formulaic it is translatable. The formula is a good tool for establishing an echo of the original in the translation. We are also greatly helped by the fact that the folktale is a kind of universal genre whose narrative motifs and tale types are shared by traditions that stretch from India to Ireland and North and South America, with the Arabic tradition sitting at the strategic centre of this geographic expanse, acting as a bridge in the transmission of folktales and sharing in the pool of available plots and motifs. There are very few Indo-European plots or narrative motifs that do not have equivalents in the various Arab traditions, and vice versa (for a comprehensive motif-index of the Arabic folktale, see El-Shamy, 1995). The conclusion to be drawn from the existence of this unified world tradition is that movement through translation across linguistic and cultural boundaries does not, in terms of the genre, necessarily entail movement across semiotic boundaries. Whether in Arabic or English there is a recognisable folktale style, a fact which invests the folktale with a high degree of translatability, and this very translatability, along with what I have called the 'contamination' of the oral by the literate, may have had a large part to play in the diffusion of the genre across cultures. As a result, the translation should aim as much for a target *style* as for a target language.

Style and Performance

Granting validity to the hypothesis that, rather any 'single, absolute difference between speech and writing in English', there are only 'dimensions of variation' (Chafe & Tannen, 1987: 390; more on variation below) the translation could then draw on the dimensions of written discourse that most approximate, or echo, speech. For the translator the assumption of responsibility to an audience therefore connotes the production of a text that reads comfortably and sounds 'natural' without violating the norms of folktale style as generally recognised within the community or destroying the features that endow the original text with its particular quality.

In discussing the elements of style in the Palestinian folktale, we need to address an aspect of performance that has a significant bearing on readability and translation, namely, the narrator's disclaimer of competence as a teller. Fatme Abd el-Qader, the narrator of the tale discussed below, is a passive bearer of the tradition who knows many folktales but refrains from telling them at social or family gatherings. When first approached she claimed she did not know any folktales and that, in any case, she did not know how to tell them well. Performance theory teaches us that this disclaimer is one of the 'keys' of performance. The concept of the key is essential to this theory and consequently to our analysis of oral style, and we shall be discussing other such keys in due course. The significant point for translation here is that we are dealing with the speech of a woman who claims she does not know how to speak well. We cannot take the narrator at her word, for the disclaimer is basically a traditional concession 'to standards of etiquette and decorum, where assertiveness is disvalued' (Bauman, 1977: 23). Though folktales serve an important function in the socialisation of children and in acquainting them with their culture, the purpose of the disclaimer is to put brackets around the act of narration itself, rendering it discursively ambiguous and affirming its amateur status. It prompts listeners to treat it as a form of play, and of course, as we know from the activity of, say, telling political jokes, play is serious business. Here we are faced with a possible contradiction; while the teller can be playful, translation itself is not necessarily a form of play, and it would be ludicrous for the translator to disclaim linguistic competence. The teller's disclaimer is part of the existential context of performance, and there is no way to recover in print the tentativeness of oral narration. All a translator can do in this case is to take advantage of what Hatim and Mason consider the 'inherent fuzziness' of linguistic registers to communicate as much of this spirit of playfulness as the target style will allow (1990: 51). This is not as difficult to achieve as it might appear at first because this play is incorporated in the text itself by various linguistic and pragmatic means, many of which lend themselves comfortably to translation (further discussion below).

Translating Style

We now turn to a specific example of text from *M&K*. The teller's performance here, as everywhere else in Palestine, consists primarily in the deployment or adaptation of the communicative resources of the dialect, the 'culture-specific constellations of communicative means' (Bauman, 1977: 22), to the needs of the genre. The disclaimer of competence in performance serves to strip away any attribution of originality to the narrator. Fatme received the tale from her mother, and she is not necessarily even using her own words. She is typical of the majority of women tellers in Palestine in that she cannot read or write and has lived all her life in the same village where she was born. Nearly 60 years old when she narrated the tale in 1977, her narrative style therefore belongs to a purely oral tradition which, with the spread of literacy, is rapidly disappearing from the country.

1 *kaanat   huun huun hal-mara,   laa btiHbal   walaa bitjiib*
   There was here, here, this woman; she does not get pregnant, and she does not bring forth.

2 *yuum   yuum,   aja 'abaal-ha,   bid-ha wlaad.*
   One day, one day, she had a desire, she wants children.

3 *qaalat,   'yaa rabbii liish   ana   'an duun ha-nnaas   hiikaa?*
   She said, 'O my Lord, why am I not like other people this way.

4 *'lawwaah 'aHbal w-a-jiib,   w-'alla   yiT 'am-nii*
   If only I get pregnant and bring forth, and may Allah feed me
   bint,   wa-law inn-haa t-kuun ṭunjara'
   'a daughter, even if she's   a cooking pot!'

5 *yuum   yuum,   qaam-at Hiblit.   ruuH ya yuum ta' ya yuum,*
   One day, one day, she up and got pregnant. Go O one day! Come O one day!
   willa   hii Saarat bid-ha t-jiib.
   and lo! she was about to deliver.

6 *qa 'dat   it-qaasi   u-ba'd   u-ba'diin   jaabat,   willa hii*
   She went into labour, and then, and then again, she delivered. And behold!
   Tunjara.   shuu bid-ha tsaawii,   Haziine?
   It was a cooking pot. What is she going to do? Sad woman!

7   *ghassalat-haa u-nazzafat-haa mliiH, u-HaTTat iTbaqiT-ha 'aliihaa,*
    She washed it and cleaned it well   and put its lid on it
    u-HaTTat- haa 'alaa ha-rraff.
    and put it   on this shelf.

8   *yuum   yuum,   willa hii ha-TTunjara b-tiHkii.*
    One day, one day, and lo! this cooking pot is speaking.

There was once a woman who could not get pregnant and have children. Once upon a day she had an urge; she wanted babies. 'O Lord!' she cried out, 'Why of all women am I like this? Would that I could get pregnant and have a baby, and may Allah grant me a girl even if she is only a cooking pot!' One day she became pregnant. A day came and a day went, and behold! she was ready to deliver. She went into labour and delivered, giving birth to a cooking pot. What was the poor woman to do? She washed it, cleaning it well, put the lid on it, and placed it on the shelf. (*M&K*: 55)

The dialect places the sample in Palestine, with certain characteristics that mark it as women's speech, among which are the glottalisation – not indicated in transcription – of the voiceless uvular stop /q/, fully articulated in male speech in the region of the Galilee; the lexical item *'lawwaah* ('would that' – *yaa riitnii* in central and southern Palestine); and the self-pitying tone which gives rise to the invocation (*du'aa', would that . . .*). The repetition of the lexical items in 1, 2, 5, 6 and 8 demonstrates a highly developed consciousness of sound values: *huun, huun* is euphonious with respect to itself, and echoic with respect to other such repetitions in the passage (*yuum yuum, ba'd u-ba'diin*). The stylistic function of this repetition is to establish a narrative rhythm based on the balanced pair in which the first pair is lexical (*there was* here, here *this woman*) and the second, clausal (*she does not get pregnant and have children*). The pattern established with the first repetition of *huun* is carried throughout. The second sentence again starts with a lexical repetition ('one day', 'one day') and enacts a clausal doubling (*she had a desire; she wants babies*), and the third embeds a clausal doubling within a clause that is already based on a pair, 'Would that I could get pregnant and have a baby, and may Allah grant me a girl even if she is only a cooking pot' (*'lawwaah aHbal wa-jiib, w-alla y-iT'am-nii bint, wa-law inn-ha t-kuun Tunjara* – note here the sound harmonies established around the semivowel /w/). With other tellers, and with Fatme in other places, a syntactic rhythm is frequently established on the basis of the repetition of three items rather than two. In such cases the syntax becomes an icon of the action because three-fold repetition is one of the basic tropes of plot in folktales. A formula has to be repeated three times to be effective, as in the complex series of modal clauses just cited, a hero must try three times before he succeeds, etc. Occasionally, as in 7, a syntactic pattern is based on four-fold repetition, and here it would be logical to assume that a two-fold pattern is being repeated twice.

As can be seen in this example, performance means that folktale style is a dynamic interplay between the highly conventional and formulaic style received from tradition and the creativity of the individual narrator. Not all narrators are equally competent, or equally creative, but since there is an acknowledged folktale style, it should be theoretically possible to recover in translation at least some of the individual features that distinguish the narrative style of one teller from another. Clearly, the feature that best characterises this style and is most conducive to readability is narrative rhythm, and the principal trait of this rhythm is a verbal economy that combines repetition with variation (of course it makes perfect sense that repetition and variation should characterise folktale style because they are the two elements best suited to hold a child's attention. Children love repetition, but they are easily bored; hence the need for variation). These roughly correspond to the syntagmatic and paradigmatic levels of analysis, and it would be safe to assume that the source of the repetition is the tradition, while variation represents the art of the individual narrator. Repetition and variation are major tropes, or keys, of Palestinian folk narrative performance, and it is their combination which gives rise to the characteristic narrative rhythm we seek to duplicate in translation. To illustrate with a preliminary example, we turn to the relative pronoun *who* in the first sentence. In oral narration dramatic impact is achieved by verbal concision. One could search an entire corpus of folktales and hardly find a relative pronoun. Would it have been better then to chop up the single utterance into two independent clauses separated either by a full stop or a semicolon: 'There was once a woman. She could not get pregnant and have children?' If this method of translation were adopted, the effect would not be dramatic impact but an extremely choppy and therefore unreadable text. Since we put the emphasis on readability from the start, it seemed wiser to place the relative pronoun, which does not receive stress in any case, in the silent spot between the two clauses; in English relative pronouns and articles are hardly visible. However, an attempt was made to preserve, in the break introduced in the second clause ('Once upon a day she had an urge; she wanted babies'), the sense of rhythm established in the first but lost in translation.

Literal translation demonstrates a basic problem in the comparative stylistics of oral texts. Parataxis is a significant key in the discursive economy of folk narrative, but it cannot be reproduced without creating a choppy text whose rhythms are not suitable to written discourse (on parataxis and hypotaxis, see Henkin, 1996). In the Arabic original the narrative presents a series of actions represented by verbs whose subjects are attached at the end as third-person pronoun morphemes, while in the translation the sequence consists of a series of subjects followed by their verbs: 'There was here here this woman. She could not get pregnant and have children. One day she had a desire; she wanted babies. She said . . .' This type of writing suffers from a stylistic defect which has been called *excessive predication*. This phenomenon is frequently encountered in folktale translations, which are either careless or carried out under the mistaken impression that faithfulness to an original is best represented by literal translation. In a literal, excessively predicated text, English word order and the visual separation of the subject from the verb imposed by the lexico-grammatical system of the language bring about a reversal of the theme/rheme relationship in the source style, and therefore a reversal in the semantic universe created by the narration. In the original Arabic the action is foregrounded and the actor relegated to the status of a verbal appendage, while in the translation the actor is foregrounded and the action is given secondary status.

Yet in oral delivery the paratactic syntax is not monotonous; rather, it serves the dramatic function in the economy of the narrative by bringing the action to the foreground, putting it in front of the audience in a sequence of verbs. Further, the presence of the narrator and the variation in the types of discourse introduced into the narration militate against monotony. A translator on the other hand is not accorded the privilege of inserting his or her own voice in the narrative; the space of the page does not represent a stage in the same manner that the space which includes narrator and audience can be thought of as a stage. To accommodate the criterion of readability, the only way out of this impasse is to create variety in word order and clause structure, maintaining the paratactic rhythm in regard to the number of actions presented but not the manner of presentation. However, before we even get to that stage we must make a major decision concerning punctuation, for the oral text is punctuated by the narrator's pauses, and punctuation provides the only orthographic clue as to how a written passage is to be read. I have alluded to this question in passing with reference to the break inserted in 2 ('Once upon a day she had an urge; she wanted babies'), but the discussion already assumed a sentence division there. In the great majority of cases, there is no problem where to insert the break: the syntax and the semantics of the narrative will provide the necessary information. But we cannot deny that the whole question of introducing punctuation into an oral text is already another form of 'contamination' by the syntax of the written language as well as the print medium. The 'oral' and the 'literate' in this case coexist as mutually reinforcing aspects of each other, rather than as two separate ontological states, for in the process of rendering an oral text into print we immediately search for the most suitable way to punctuate, and conversely, in punctuating we keep an ear open to the rhythms of the original. Hence Benjamin's notion of the echo works not only in translation across languages, but also in the movement from an oral to a printed text. In ambiguous cases the fact of having to render the oral text into another language will be the deciding factor; in such a case 'contamination' is introduced not only by the print medium but also by the target style itself.

The folktale, being an oral genre, also grants the narrator much freedom in the use of interruptive structures – structures that do not belong to the grammar of the discourse as such but serve to heighten the dramatic impact of the narrative. The interruptive key, one of the most important communicative means available to tellers for creating a dramatic effect and evoking wonder, springs from the living voice of the narrator in performance. It may take the form of interjections (*u-shuu* – and what?), exclamations (*willa* – and behold!), rhetorical questions (*shuu bid-haa t-saawii* – What is she going to do?), invocations (*Hashaak* – Save your honor! [upon the mention of a socially undesirable subject]), and editorial comments (*Haziine* 'poor woman!'), or of direct address to the audience (*u-ba'diin ya Habibiinii* – and then, my little darlings). True, repetition is available to male as well as female tellers, but the frequent and artistic use of these interruptive structures, particularly the invocatory ones, is more characteristic of women's speech than men's. While excessive use indicates an immature narrator, scant use renders the narration flat and lifeless. This balance must also be kept in the translation so as to maintain the individual style of each narrator and the tone of wonder on which the art of the folktale is based.

Returning now to the example, we see that in 1 ('There was once a woman who could not get pregnant and have children') and 2 ('Once upon a day she had an urge; she wanted babies') the grammar of the clauses reproduces the original. In 3 ('O Lord!' she cried out, 'Why of all women am I like this?') the word order has been changed, taking advantage of the conventions for rendering dialogue in print to create rhythmic variety and avoid an excessively predicated texture. Sentence 4 ('Would that I could get pregnant and have a baby, and may Allah grant me a girl even if she is only a cooking pot!') has the same clause division as the original and follows its parallelism closely. In 5 ('One day she became pregnant') there was no elegant way to recuperate the lively rhythm of double repetition, initiated by the lexical item *yuum yuum* (one day, one day) rendered as *once upon a day* and followed by the syntactic doublet *qaamat Hiblit* (she up and got pregnant), while in the second part ('A day came and a day went, and behold! she was ready to deliver') a definite attempt was made to maintain

rhythm with the insertion of the exclamatory *behold!* and by maintaining
the repetition of what Palva (1977, 1984) calls the 'descriptive imperative' –
though not in the same imperative form ('Go O one day, come O one day!'
rendered as 'A day came and a day went'). It should be noted here that the
verbs *qaamat* in *qaamat Hiblit*, *bidha* in *bidha t-jiib*, and *qa'dat* in *qa'dat it-qaasii*
are auxiliaries of aspect rather than independent verbs; they are used in this
manner to create a rhythm based on what I have called the 'doublet' and
draws directly on the characteristics of Palestinian Arabic.

The first part of 6 (*She went into labour and delivered, giving birth to a cooking
pot*) involved a compromise; the division into three clauses is based on the
division of the action into three parts (she went into labour, she delivered,
she brought forth a cooking pot), but again to avoid monotony the last verb
is given subordinate status as an *-ing* form. The compromise here is the
sacrifice of the interruptive deictic *behold!* As indicated, the rhythm of three
actions in a row is perhaps the most common in Palestinian oral narrative
(see *M&K*: 6), but the question of usage and literary context intrudes. There
is no English lexical equivalent to *willa* that does not sound either too
formal (*lo! behold!*) or too informal (*there she is!*) A formulation such as, 'She
went into labour and delivered, and behold! it was a cooking pot' sounds
like a travesty of Biblical style; it sounds more like a fake epic than a folk
narrative. Therefore, it cannot be translated every time it occurs in the
original without completely changing the tone of the narration. Sentence 7
illustrates well the dangers of excessive predication. The rhythm here is
based on a quadruplet, and if the second clause had not been converted to a
subordinating *-ing* form ('She washed it, cleaning it well, put the lid on it
and placed it on the shelf'), the resulting monotony would have been
destructive to the fluency of the translation.

My perception of performance as style rather than style as performance
springs directly from the narrative practice of Palestinian tellers as illus-
trated here (for another perspective on performance in relation to speech
production and group identity, see Muhawi, 1996). Though the language of
the example is close to that used in ordinary speech, it is as we have seen a
form of what Palva (1992) calls 'artistic colloquial Arabic', a literary
language whose sound harmonies and highly patterned syntax remove it
from the genre of ordinary conversation. Therefore, an informal, conversational style relying on the use of colloquialisms would not necessarily be
the appropriate register in English. To the extent that it is a mimetic sign of
Palestinian verbal culture, which relies heavily on speech acts characterised by repetition of ritualised expressions and politeness formulas,
folktale style will embody or enact some forms of repetition in order to
reach its audience. The repetition of *huun huun, yuum yuum, u-ba'd u-ba'diin*
(1, 2, 5, 6), for example, represents a literalisation of the Palestinian

tendency to use the dual in order to create phatic communion, as we observe in the most common greeting exchange: *marHabaa / marHabtiin* (hello! two helloes!), or in the repetition of such dual forms as *Sahtiin* (two healths! – for eating) and *ahliin* (two welcomes! for greeting upon seeing, or in response to an expression of thanks: *shukran, ahliin, ahliin* (thank you, two welcomes, two welcomes). It seems that one *ahliin*, even though it already signifies 'two thanks', does not carry sufficient weight by itself to convince the interlocutor of the sincerity of the emotion. The expression becomes pragmatically charged only with the repetition. In other words, the aesthetics of Palestinian oral narrative style draw directly upon the cultural semiotics of the Palestinian dialect, and what we have in this and other oral narrative texts is a form of mimesis, or translation, of certain (socio-pragmatic) feature of the dialect into aesthetic facts of narration.

Paradoxical as it may seem, the aesthetic function of repetition is to achieve the greatest possible verbal economy. Even the lexical repetition on which the tale opens, though apparently redundant, is in fact a highly economical means to achieve its intended pragmatic end, for the repeated items are temporal and spatial deictics ('here, here'; 'one day, one day') whose function is to create the proper atmosphere by removing the action from the lived space and temporality of the audience and creating a fictional space and temporality in their place. The inversion of the opening in English ('There was once', rather than the more conventional, 'Once upon a time there was . . .') represented an attempt to account for the unusual opening of the tale. Alternatives involving lexical repetition (e.g. 'there was, there was') were rejected as cumbersome and detrimental to the sense of the reading rhythm we are after. At the level of the clause, however, the situation is totally different because clausal repetition, when achieved with sufficient variation to avoid monotony, is a desirable criterion in written English. It would have been possible for example to divide the opening line into two sentences, depending on whether we understood there to have been a full stop between the positive statement, 'There was once a woman', and the two negations that follows. But Fatme hardly pauses at this point, intending the negation, I believe, as a qualifying clause to the affirmation. Hence, it was translated as one sentence with two clauses, including after 'who could not get pregnant' the semantically redundant but culturally and stylistically essential second negation ('and have children'). The repetition here is a perfect joining of culture and style. The purpose of getting pregnant is to have children, and in Palestinian society it is tragic for a woman not to be able to have children; hence the thought is repeated, setting the stage for the general rhythm of double repetition on which the tale opens.

We have seen to what extent the balanced syntax of Fatme's individual style creates a pattern based on repetition with roots in cultural praxis, which when combined with variation establishes an aural rhythm that must somehow be rendered in the target style. Within the semiotics of the oral narrative genre we are exploring here, the syntactic rhythm of balanced repetition falls under the category of the poetic, which is reinforced at the phonological level with a whole congeries of sound patterns expressed in ditties, poems and rhyming formulas. It is the combination of repetition with variation that supplies the key to a stylistically viable translation of this genre.

Repetition, Variation and Translation

It is the combination of repetition with variation that supplies the key to a stylistically viable translation of this genre. Repetition is discussed as a cohesive device by Halliday and Hassan (1976) under the general heading of reiteration, itself a subcategory of lexical cohesion. The basis of cohesion in oral narrative is the sequence of events, and that is managed through a variety of syntactic, rhetorical and narrative means, as well as the presence of the teller. However, lexical cohesion does contribute to one major feature of oral style, its concision. Tannen (1989) provides a comprehensive analysis of the function of repetition in oral discourse. Taking the argument considerably further than Halliday and Hassan, she concludes that repetition is a significant factor in language production itself:

> Analysis of repetition . . . sheds light on our conception of language production . . . In short, it suggests that language is less freely generated, more pre-patterned, than most current linguistic theory acknowledges. This is not, however, to say that speakers are automatons, cranking out language by rote. Rather, pre-patterning (or idomaticity, or formulaicity) is a resource for creativity. It is the play between fixity and novelty that makes possible the creation of meaning. (Tannen, 1989: 37)

It would appear that originality in the production of both language and oral narrative are parallel processes, and this no doubt has significant implications for children's acquisition of their native tongue in listening to folktales. Tannen shows that what we take to be ordinary conversation is already a highly structured activity, and we take this step further by saying that these structures provide the raw material from which oral narrative is constructed. Here we have a basis for yet another bridge between oral narrative and language: the relationship between the implicit patterns of ordinary conversation and the explicit ones that animate a folktale are mimetic, that is, artistic or aesthetic transformations of stylistic facts already existing in language. Hymes's conclusions in his analysis of Ojibway oral poetry push this relationship to an ultimate degree of closeness: he deduces linguistic structure from the structure of oral poetry. If we see repetition and variation as constitutive tropes or keys in the style of Palestinian oral narrative, he sees them as basic elements of structure in language: 'By structure I mean here particularly the form of repetition and variation, of constants and contrasts, in verbal organization' (1981: 42). Here the whole notion of mimesis, or the transformation of nature into art, is negated, for the same processes are seen to give shape to both nature (language) and art (folk narrative). 'Such structure', Hymes goes on to say, 'is manifest in linguistic form . . . [It] is the matrix of the meaning and effect of the poem' (1981: 42). These conclusions are startling in some respects, for they demonstrate to what extent stylistics and grammar are the reverse sides of the same coin. At the same time they also have significant implications to our purpose here for they provide further confirmation that a 'faithful' translation is possible not only on the grounds articulated above, but also on the more general grounds of the unity of the whole process, the seamless web that connects language with its artefacts.

Conclusion

Folktale style, though oral, is not spontaneous like conversation; nor is it improvised like personal narratives. As we see from our example, folktale orality is highly mannered, replete with grammatical, rhetorical, and narrative patterns of all sorts. We might say that this kind of patterning– which is responsible for the durability, formal stability and wide geographic spread of the folktale – endows it with the formal characteristics of writing. It is as if orality in the folktale, by virtue of its form, is already contaminated by writing. Oral literature, Chafe argues, resembles writing more than it does spoken language.

> The permanence, value, and polish of an oral text may lead to a more integrated, less fragmented kind of language than that found in spontaneous conversation, and the detachment of a reciter from his audience may produce a kind of language lacking the involvement of colloquial speech. (1982: 52)

Of course in folktale narration the teller is not involved directly with the audience; the genre stands between them. Chafe concludes that oral literature has 'a kind of permanence analogous to that of written language' (1982: 52). After all, there is no way to tell the age of any given folktale; but we can reasonably conjecture that folktales told today may be as old, or older, than any available written stories. The degree of similarity or difference between oral and written discourse has been argued back and forth in the literature, but our analysis has shown that orality is not limited to, or defined solely by, speech events, as there are oral elements in all discourse, whether spoken or written. And literacy is not strictly defined chirographically, either in terms of manuscript or print culture, for the highly elaborate grammar of any language is already a form of literacy, just as the conventions of folk narrative, orally transmitted from one generation to another, also represent a kind of literacy. Our conclusion therefore is that the folktale as a genre lies between prose and poetry, between orality and literacy, and here lies its potential for translatability.

CHAPTER 8

The Qur'an: Limits of Translatability

HUSSEIN ABDUL-RAOF

Introduction

According to Muslim tradition, God bestows miracles upon His Prophets. Each miracle represents a challenge to the prevalent skill in which each Prophet's people excelled. For instance, the miracle of Moses was an apparent sorcery since this was common at his time, and the miracle of Jesus was the power to heal since medicine and healing were prevalent then. For the Prophet Muhammad, the dominant skill was literary ability: linguistic competence echoed by poetry and oratory skills were highly competitive among Arab tribes. The Arabs were infatuated by the use of their language; it was employed as a 'weapon' against enemy tribes, with some poets composing the greatest poetry Arabic has to offer. For this very reason, the Qur'an is considered by Muslim scholars as the miracle of Muhammad.

The purpose of this chapter is not to discuss the theological aspects of the Qur'an as a miracle; rather, it explores Qur'anic discourse, its linguistic idiosyncrasies and prototypical features that have challenged the limits of translatability. The discussion focuses on linguistic and semantic, structural and stylistic, rhetorical, and cultural voids – notoriously translation-resistant – that emerge in the translation of the Qur'an into English. The discussion in this chapter is however applicable to other target languages.

Limits of Translatability

During the Prophet Muhammad's era, the translation of the Qur'an was limited to diplomatic purposes. Some companions spoke other languages such as Suhaib and Salman who spoke Greek and Farsi respectively. Envoys were sent to neighbouring countries where they rendered some of the Qur'an in the local languages to rulers: Ja'far b. Abi Talib read Chapter 19 to the Emperor of Abyssinia and a letter sent to the Emperor of the Roman Empire included some translated Qur'anic statements. On the theological level, the translation of the Qur'an was a controversial issue. The Muslim scholar Imam Abu Hanifah, for example, sanctioned the reading of *al-FaatiHa* (the Opening – chapter 1) in its translated form in any language in prayers. His *fatwa* (ruling) was, however, withdrawn soon after, and the consensus among Muslim scholars has since been to read the Qur'an during prayers in its Arabic original by Arab and non-Arab Muslims alike.

The translation of the Qur'an has been traditionally rejected by Muslim scholars (cf. al-Qattan, 1990). Only exegetical translation is allowed, that is translation based on commentary and explication of the Qur'anic text. Since 'no translation is entirely 'acceptable' or entirely 'adequate'' (Toury, 1980: 49), a translation of the Qur'an 'is not the Qur'an and can never be' (Turner, 1997: xiv). The change in word order and the subsequent semantic change in the target language have led some Muslim scholars, such as Muhammad Shakir, of al-Azhar Mosque in Egypt, to oppose the translation of the Qur'an into foreign languages. Shakir (1926: 163) states that in the matter of the lawfulness of translating the holy Qur'an into any foreign language, we can have little confidence in the balance of meaning being preserved, as we can have in regard to the changing of the order and the arrangement of words within the sacred text itself.

Qur'anic discourse is a linguistic scenery characterised by a rainbow of syntactic, semantic, rhetorical, phonetic and cultural features that are distinct from other types of Arabic discourse. Through the coalition of these features, a unique linguistic texture unfolds to the reader dominated by harmony on the syntactic, semantic and prosodic levels: in fact interfertilisation among these elements could not be better achieved. Most of these features are alien to the linguistic norms of other languages. The frequent use of shift in tense or person, for instance, is employed in Qur'anic discourse as a linguistic means to achieve what Longacre (1983: 28) calls 'heightened vividness'. This may be obtained by a shift in the nominal/verbal balance, a tense shift, a shift from third person to second person and then back to first person, a shift from plural to singular within a given person, or by using rhetorical questions. The following example illustrates a unique shift in person (full and partial citations from the Qur'an are represented by chapter and verse numbers (10:16), for example, throughout this chapter).

1   wa man yu'min bil-lahi wa ya`mal SaaliHan yudkhilhu jannaatin tajrii min taHtiha l'anhaaru khaalidiina fiihaa qad 'aHsana l-laahu lahu rizqan (65:11)

God will show anyone who believes in Him (God) and acts honorably into gardens through which rivers flow, to live there forever. What a handsome provision God has granted him! (Irving, 1985: 333)

Here, we have the third person singular pronoun in the words *yu'min* (he believes), *ya'mal* (he acts), *yudkhil* (He (God) shows to the way to), third person plural in the word *khaalidiina* (they live there for ever), and then a third person singular in the word *lahu* (for him). This is a linguistic mechanism particularly common in Qur'anic discourse with the goal of achieving heightened vividness, a sublime style and mental preparedness, by making the reader alert to the message conveyed by the statement. Qur'an-specific linguistic features pose serious challenges for the translator and translation theories. Equivalence, still an important principle in translation studies, is dramatically underachieved and, in some cases, not achieved at all in Qur'an translations. Guillaume (1990: 73) rightly claims that the Qur'an is one of the world's classics, which cannot be translated without grave loss. It has a rhythm of peculiar beauty and a cadence that charms the ear. As the following discussion shows, English translations of the Qur'an provide neither cadence nor linguistic beauty.

Available Qur'an translations have either adopted a semantic or a communicative translation. A semantic translation attempts to render, as closely as the semantic and syntactic structures of the target language allow, the exact contextual meaning of the source language message. A communicative translation, however, attempts to produce on its readers an effect as close as possible to that obtained on the reader of the source text. Arabic and English are linguistically and culturally incongruous languages; and a literal translation of a text like the Qur'an easily leads either to ambiguity, skewing of the source text intentionality, or inaccuracy in rendering the source message to the target language reader.

Lexical and Semantic Voids

Some Qur'anic lexical items are pregnant with Qur'an-specific emotive overtones, which in turn create lexical voids in translation. The lexical compression of Qur'anic expressions can only be tackled through componential analysis: the translator's nightmare can be alleviated by the semantic decomposition of the words. As such, a periphrastic translation approach needs to be adopted because English cannot penetrate Qur'anic lexical and morphological defences. Consider examples 2, 3 and 4.

2   *tayammum* (4:43): to strike your hands on the earth and pass the palm of each hand on the back of the other and then blow off the dust from them and pass (rub) them on your face. It is a kind of ablution that is adopted when someone is spiritually unclean and there is no water.

3   *mawquudha* (5:3): any animal that receives a violent blow, is left to die, and then eaten without being slaughtered according to Islamic law.

4   *kazhiim* (12:84): to fall into silent melancholy, to be filled with grief but not to complain to any one except to your Lord.

Some Qur'anic expressions reflect sensitive meaning geared towards the core of the Islamic faith as in 5.

5   *aS-Samad* (102:2): God the eternal, the uncaused cause of all being.

This Qur'anic expression signifies the notion of *aS-Samadiyya* which designates the total perfection of might, power, wisdom, knowledge, honour, and lordship of Almighty God, the need of others for Him while the reverse is not true (see ibn Kathir, 1993). Qur'an translators have expressed their frustration with the dilemma of rendering this expression. Ali (1983), for example, admits that it is difficult to translate it by one word, and Asad (1980) acknowledges that his rendering gives no more than an approximate meaning for the word.

The morphological mechanism of Arabic enables it to produce lexical items derived from the same root (theoretically over 200 words can be derived from the same root). The accurate meaning of the Arabic word produced is often difficult to be achieved through a one-word target language. The Arabic lexical void needs to be paraphrased, as in examples 6, 7, 8 and 9.

6   *al-budna* (22:38): cows, oxen or camels driven to be offered as sacrifices by the pilgrims at the sanctuary of Mecca.

7   *yastami'* (26:25 and 39:18) meaning 'to make an effort in order to listen attentively and comprehend what you hear', and is derived from the word *sama'a* (to hear).

8   *al-muD'ifuun* (30:39): those who will get a multiplied recompense.

9   *yaSTarikh* (35:37): crying with pain and appealing loudly for help. This is derived from the root word *Sarakha* (to shout).

Some lexical gaps express Qur'anic concepts that cannot be matched by the target language, such as *taqwaa* and *khushuu'* in 10.

10   dhaalika l-kitaabu laa rayba fiihi hudan lil-muttaqiin (2:2)

     This is the Book; in it is guidance sure, without doubt, for those who fear God. (Ali, 1983: 17)

In this verse, the word *muttaqiin* is inappropriately rendered as 'those who fear God'. Ali provides a different 'inaccurate' meaning for the same word elsewhere in the Qur'an (16:128) 'those who restrain themselves' (ibid.: 690). To avoid the loss of its sensitive overtones in Arabic, other Qur'an translators merely transliterated this expression. Hilali and Khan (1983: 3) give a periphrastic translation after the transliteration, 'the pious and righteous persons who fear Allah much, perform all kinds of good deeds which he has forbidden, and love Allah much, perform all kinds of goods deeds which he has ordained.' Thus, *taqwaa* does not mean 'fear of God' only, but it is a Qur'anic notion which combines many spiritual aspects including fear and love of God. Similarly, the translation of the Qur'an-specific expression *khushuu'* (*khaashi'iin*, the performers of *khushuu'*) leads to lexical voids in English. As the translation of 11 shows, it is only through periphrastic translation that the concept of *khushuu'* can be approximately captured.

11   wa 'innahaa lakabiiratun 'illa 'ala l-khaashi'iin (2:45)

And truly it is extremely heavy and hard except for *al-khashi'un* (the true believers in Allah) those who obey Allah with full submission, fear much from his punishment and believe in His promise (paradise) and in His warning (hell). (al-Hilali and Khan, 1983: 11)

One language can be semantically more specific than another. This linguistic specificity can be achieved either through the lexicon or the morphological system of the language. English, for instance, is semantically more specific than Arabic in the description of military actions like 'shelling' and 'bombardment', as the action of shelling is not the same as that of bombardment. Arabic, however, does not distinguish between the two acts unless more words, i.e. through paraphrasing, are added. Arabic has only one word *qaSf* for the two English expressions, but it supplements the specific meanings by the addition of a descriptive word. Thus 'shelling' is *qaSf bil-madfa'iyya* and 'bombardment' is *qaSf biT-Taa'iraat*. Conversely, Arabic can be more specific than English. Morphologically related expressions have semantic subtleties that can only be accounted for through the paraphrasing of the semantic void, as in 12.

12   nazzala 'alayka l-kitaaba bil-Haqqi muSaddiqan limaa bayna yadayhi wa 'anzala t-tawraata wa l-'injiila. (3:3)

It is He who sent down to you (step by step) in truth, the Book, confirming what went before it, and He sent down the Law (of Moses) and the Gospel (of Jesus).

The word *nazzala* creates a semantic void as it signifies the piecemeal revelation of the Qur'an that lasted 23 years. By contrast, the word '*anzala* means 'to reveal in one go and at once'. Thus, a distinction is made between the two kinds of revelation: the piecemeal revelation of the Qur'an and the singular revelation of the Torah and the Gospel. To appreciate the nuances of Qur'anic discourse on the lexical level, consider example 13 in which the semantic subtleties are vividly expressed through two lexical items which may look similar to the reader but whose componential features are drastically distinct.

13   huwa l-ladhii ja'ala sh-shamsa Diyaa'an wa l-qamara nuuran (10:5)

It is He who made the sun to be a shining glory and the moon to be a light. (Ali, 1983: 484)

Although the words *Diyaa'an* and *nuuran* seem to be synonyms, the two signify distinct semantic properties in this Qur'anic statement. *Diyaa'an* is not captured by the translation 'shining glory' because its meaning 'the generation of heat' is not echoed; hence the requirement for an informative periphrastic translation. The word *nuuran*, however, is appropriately rendered as 'light', perhaps by coincidence, signifying 'non-generation of heat but light only'.

Some lexical voids cannot even be paraphrased. For example, the lexical item *duuni*, in 14, co-occurs with false gods compared to God, and the closest approximations given by all Qur'an translators for this item are 'beside, besides, instead of'.

14   qul 'ud'uu l-ladhiina za'amtum min duuni l-laahi (34:22)

Say: 'Appeal to those whom you claim to instead of to God.' (Irving, 1985: 238)

The word *duuni* signifies dignity, might and monotheism, meaning there is nothing 'above' God or 'equal' to Him.

Structural/Stylistic Voids

The syntactic structures represent the linguistic patterns of a given language; the constituents of a pattern are lexical items of different grammatical functions, such as nouns, verbs, adjectives, particles, etc. Although the permutation of constituents is fairly fixed in a given language, we do encounter a variety of word orders that may be employed to produce effective and sublime styles. These word orders are usually semantically oriented and their meaning is distinct from that of normal word order. On the other hand, the selection of certain lexical items – or rather the selection of a specific grammatical form of the chosen lexical item – dictates semantic subtleties whose delicate underlying meanings can be quite difficult to tackle through translation.

Qur'anic discourse is characterised by highly specific syntactic and lexical items. Both the word order and the selection of specific lexical items are semantically oriented. In addition, stylistic and syntactic properties are language-specific and may not be shared by other languages. The foregrounding (clefting) of certain constituents in Qur'anic discourse has a special communicative function. Foregrounding is a syntactic operation that places one or more constituents sentence-initially for effective stylistic reasons. Thus, syntax and style stand 'shoulder to shoulder' to produce the desired communicative goal whose meaning would not have been achieved via an ordinary simple syntactic pattern. Style and meaning are inextricably linked, with the former contributing to or even creating the latter (Adab, 1996). Some Qur'an translations, like that of Ali (1983), are regarded as text-centred because the translator is constantly 'loyal' to the source text. This type of translation applies to syntactic structures that exhibit foregrounding of constituents.

15 min nuTfatin khalaqahu. (80:19)

From a sperm-drop He hath created him. (Ali, 1983: 1689)

The translator manages to render the Qur'anic structure but at the expense of the syntactic norms of English. Consequently, his translation sounds formally biased and the patterns archaic. The aim behind Ali's translation strategy is to preserve the Qur'anic text tone, its splendour and stylistic specialty. The intentionality of the text can be echoed by the stylistic variations through foregrounding, for instance, in order to highlight a particular notion in a given statement. In the above example, the foregrounded element is the prepositional phrase *min nuTfatin* 'from a sperm-drop'.

Asad (1980: 928), however, ignores the importance of the foregrounded constituents in structures like 15 above and opts for a different word order. But Qur'an translators need to realise that foregrounded Qur'anic elements have a particular communicative function in the hierarchy of the text levels (see Bell, 1991).

Generally, the syntactic norms of the target language fail to match those of Qur'anic discourse.

16 fa'awjasa fii nafsihi khiifatan Muusaa (20:67)

So Moses conceived is his mind a (sort of) fear. (Ali, 1983: 803)

In the Arabic, the subject, Moses, is backgrounded (placed at the end of the statement) while in the English translation, it is foregrounded (placed sentence-initially). While there is a certain consensus that it is often possible to achieve a fairly good degree of resemblance in semantic representation across languages, the same cannot be said of stylistic properties, which often consist of linguistic features that are far from universal (see Gutt, 1991).

If we examine structures such as those found in 17, we notice the correlation between meaning and Qur'anic style:

17 'innanii 'ana l-laahu laa 'ilaaha 'illaa 'anaa fa-'budnii (20:14)

> Verily I am God; there is no god but I; therefore serve Me. (Arberry, 1980: 340)

This Qur'anic structure may, from a surface structure point of view, look too long for its intended message: it has pronouns unnecessarily repeated *'innanii, 'ana, 'anaa* which, in fact, all refer to the same referent *l-laahu*. This, however, is not without a good semantic reason; there are two separate but interrelated propositions relayed via this Qur'anic style: the first proposition is about knowing God and His existence (*'innanii 'ana l-laahu*) followed by the second proposition which is about knowing the oneness of God and that He alone is worthy of worship (*laa 'ilaaha 'illaa 'anaa fa-'budnii*). The use of the cohesive tie *fa* before the verb *'budnii* (serve or worship me) also has a semantic function: immediate action with no hesitation, i.e. to execute the action verb to worship at once.

The correlation between style and meaning in the Qur'an is semantically motivated and at times translation-resistant (see Ithima, 1972).

18 yawma tajidu kullu nafsin maa 'amilat min khayrin muHzharan wa maa 'amilat min suu'in. (3:30)

> On the day when every soul will find itself confronted with all that it hath done of good and all that it hath done of evil. (Pickthall, 1969: 70)

The appropriate way to demonstrate stylistic loss in the translation of 18 is through a back translation of the English version: *yawma tajidu kullu nafsin maa 'amilat min khayrin wa suu'in muHzharan* (On the day when every soul will find itself confronted with all it has done of good and evil). The back translation shows the inability of the target language to maintain the semantically oriented Qur'anic style. The intended message has been impaired due to the limitations by the linguistic and stylistic norms of the English language. A careful linguistic investigation of the above Qur'anic structure reveals the value of the buffer word *muHzharan* (be confronted with) which separates the two clauses *maa 'amilat min khayrin* and *maa 'amilat min suu'in*. Without separating the two clauses with the buffer word, the meaning of the Qur'anic structure will be affected.

The word order, i.e. *nazhm* (the special arrangement of words) also has both a semantic and a rhetorical function in every Qur'anic communicative event (abu Musa, 1988). Word order, according to St. Jerome (Schwarz, 1955: 50), contains a mystery transcending human understanding. This view has been taken too literally by Ali (1983: 1222) who renders *tis'un wa tis'uuna*, for example, literally as 'nine and ninety' rather than ninety nine. Ali not only retains source text style to the detriment of the target text syntax and style, but he has also been unsuccessful in preserving the unique Qur'an-bound hysteron and proteron style. Consider 19 where the word *faqiirun* (in – desperate – need) is backgrounded, but turned into a foregrounded element in the translation.

19   rabbi ''innii limaa 'anzalta 'ilayya min khayrin faqiirun. (28:24)

O my Lord! Truly am I in (desperate) need of any good that Thou dost send me! (Ali, 1983: 1008)

It is through word order that we can achieve an oxymoron effect where two antonyms stand next to each other so that their opposite meanings stand out.

20   sayaj'alu l-laahu ba`da 'usrin yusraa. (65:7)

After difficulty, God will soon grant relief. (Ali, 1983: 1565)

The oxymoron words are *'usrin* and *yusraa* (difficulty and relief). Qur'anic word order has not been maintained in the target text which, as a consequence, has lost this stylistic feature.

21   li-ladhiina laa yu'minuuna bi-l'aakhirati mathalu s-saw'i wa li-llaahi l-mathalu l-'a'laa. (16:60)

The similitude of evil applies to those who do not believe in the Hereafter, while the similitude of good applies to those who do believe. However, the highest and best similitude of all applies to God. (Turner, 1997: 159)

The translation of 21 shows loss of stylistic effect when the source text antithesis is wasted and not appropriately compensated for. This and other examples show that Qur'an translation, in general, suffers from over-translation, loss of form, change in word order, and exhibits what Kievit (1990: 319–20) calls 'target accommodation' (the adaptation of a translation towards the target readership) and 'stylistic accommodation' (when the source text undergoes flattening). In 21, Turner (1997) fronts the backgrounded subject noun phrases *mathalu s-saw'i* (the similitude of evil) and *l-mathalu l-'a'laa* (best similitude of all), i.e. he places them sentence-initially in the target text. He uses the strategy of 'rephrasing' (Lorscher, 1991: 113) where a problematic source language text segment is tackled by changing its form (surface structure) but keeping its meaning invariant as far as possible. Further, this example shows the unnecessary 'over-translation' or periphrasis (while the similitude of good applies to those who do believe) which is not provided in the source text. It is perhaps provided to ease accessibility and intelligibility for the target language readers.

The stylistic mechanism of word order in Qur'anic discourse is a semantic requirement. In other words, word order is semantically motivated and there are communicative goals to be achieved out of a given marked order that involves foregrounding of a lexical item.

22 wa ja'aluu li-llaahi shurakaa'a l-jinna. (6:100)

Yet they make the Jinns equals with God. (Ali, 1983: 319)

The Arabic is mainly characterised by a semantically motivated fore-grounding feature where the lexical item first object *l-jinna* (the Jinns) is taken out of its post-verbal position and placed sentence-finally while *li-llaahi* (with God) has been taken from its original sentence-final position and placed post-verbally for important communicative reasons. This is a marked word order whose normal unmarked one is: *wa ja'aluu l-jinna shurakaa'a li-llaahi* (they made jinns equal with God). The target text, however, is no more than a 'crude' approximation of the latter ordinary unmarked Arabic (non-Qur'anic) word order. By foregrounding *li-llahi* and backgrounding *l-jinna*, the marked Qur'anic structure has fulfilled four communicative goals: (1) disapprobation of what the unbelievers say, (2) bringing to the attention of the reader the notion of calumny that the unbelievers usually attribute to God, (3) deploring and condemning the association of others with God, and (4) preserving the supreme status of God as Creator by foregrounding *li-llahi* and placing it before *l-jinna*, thus showing the ordinary status of the Jinns who are themselves created by God (cf. al-Zayn, 1985; al-Zamakhshari, 1995; al-Qurtubi, 1997). These communicative goals are realised by the marked exotic Qur'anic word order, which has been relinquished and cannot be adequately captured in the translation due to stylistic and word order requirements of the target language.

Languages arrange their words in *order* – some rigidly, others much more freely (see Beekman and Callow, 1974). What is often not realised is that word order in itself can convey meaning. An interesting example of a semantically oriented word order in Qur'anic discourse is:

23 'inna raHmata l-laahi qariibun mina l-muHsiniina. (7:56)

For the mercy of God is (always) near to those who do good. (Asad, 1980: 356)

The intentionality of the source text producer is to provide a syntactic structure in which the word *l-laahi* (God) is not surrounded by two feminine words. Thus, the word *qariibun* (near) is given the masculine form although it describes the word *raHmata* (mercy) which is feminine and whose descriptive word should also be feminine, according to normal Arabic usage. To maintain the underpinning Qur'anic notion of monotheism and to refute pre-Islamic and pagan beliefs, the word *Allah* always appears in the singular and is placed next to masculine nouns. This Qur'an-specific structure causes syntactic gaps that cannot be easily plugged in translation.

Semantico-stylistic effects in Qur'anic discourse constitute another example of un-translatability. Oath, for instance, in classical Arabic is regarded as a stylistic ornament and an indication of a highly elaborate style through which the prepositional content of a given verb is stressed and highlighted to the reader/listener. The semantic content of the verb is emphasised through two means of stress, or *stress tools*, that accompany the verb: the letters *li* and *nna* are used as *stress tools* for semantic purposes. Such language-specific semantic and stylistic subtleties cannot be easily captured in English translation.

24   ta-llaahi la'akiidanna 'aSnaamakum. (20:57)

And by God, I have a plan for your idols. (Asad, 1980: 835)

Here, the verb *'akiid* (have a plan) is stressed and brought to the reader's attention through the initial letter *la* cliticised onto it and also through the final letter *nna*, both of these stress means have been relinquished in the target text.

Unlike explicit oath, as in 24, implicit oath and the stress of proposition which is realised through stress tools is impossible to render into a target language like English; implicit oath is a Qur'an-bound specialty. Consider example 25.

25   wa lanbluwannakum Hattaa na'lama l-mujaahidiina minkum wa S-Saabiriina. (47:31)

And we shall try you until We test those among you who strive their utmost and persevere in patience. (Asad, 1980: 1386)

The implicit oath that still provides stylistic glitter to Qur'anic structure is lost in the linguistic environment of the target text. Stress tools in Arabic have been loosely compensated for by the non-equivalent item *shall*. Certainty of action can also be stressed and highlighted through the same stress tools, i.e. the prepositional content of the verb is stressed as in 26.

26   wa 'idh ta'adhdhana rabbukum la'in shakartum la-'aziidannakum (14:7)

And remember! Your Lord caused to be declared (publicly): 'If ye are grateful, I will add more (favors) unto you. (Asad, 1980: 621)

The translation of 26 shows a lack of the necessary stylistic mechanism and its special significance in the Qur'an. Qur'anic style emphasises, as an implicit oath, the propositional content of the verb *'aziid* and its certainty by employing an initial *la* and a final *nna*; thus we have *la-'aziidanna* which is totally distinct from the non-emphatic verb *sawfa 'aziidu* (I will add) that lacks the stylistic element of oath.

A further example that reflects Qur'an-specific stylistic patterns is 27.

27 'alam ya'lamuu 'anna l-laaha huwa yaqbalu t-tawbata 'an 'ibaadihi wa ya'khudhu S-Sadaqaati wa 'anna l-laaha huwa t-tawwaabu r-raHiimu. (9:104)

Do not they know that God does accept repentance from His votaries and receives their gifts of charity, and that God is verily He, the oft-returning, most merciful? (Ali, 1983: 472)

Here, the insertion of the third person singular pronoun *huwa* (he) twice is to achieve specificity and affirmation (*takhSiis wa ta'kiid*). This particular style provides the meaning that only God, rather than the Prophet Muhammad, has the authority to either accept or reject repentance, and that forgiveness can only be authorised by God alone (cf. al-Zamakhshari, 1995). The deletion of the pronoun *huwa* would not produce this intention of the source text.

Rhetorical Voids

Qur'anic discourse is characterised by a considerable number of rhetorical features. Among the rhetorical features whose translation imposes some limitations on the translator are:

Alliteration: This is a rhetorical ornament that adds melodic sounds to the statement and enhances cadence. Alliteration is the occurrence of identical sounds sentence-initially. In 28, this is achieved by the sound *m-*. This rhetorical (and phonetic) feature has been lost in the translation.

28 wa man 'azhlamu mi-mman mana'a masaajida l-laahi (2:114)

And who is more unjust than he who forbids from any of His houses of worship. (Asad, 1980: 24)

Antithesis: This is marked by parallelistic structures that can hardly be rendered into a target language.

29 'inna l-'abraara lafii na'iim. wa 'inna l-fujjaara lafii jaHiim. (82:13–14)

As for the righteous, they will be in Bliss; and the wicked, they will be in the fire. (Ali, 1983: 1701)

In 29, the constituents of antithesis are lexical items of parallelistic structures represented by the words *l-'abraara* (righteous) and *l-fujjaara* (wicked) and *na'iim* (bliss) and *jaHiim* (fire). The target text fails to communicate these Qur'an-specific features. These words have another rhetorical function: isocolon. Thus, two significant rhetorical effects / functions have been lost in the translation.

Metaphor: The rhetorical feature of metaphor can express a Qur'anic concept that is hard to render in another language.

30   wa min 'aayaatihi 'annaka tara l-'arDa khaashi'atan fa'idhaa 'anzalnaa 'alayha l-maa'a 'ihtazzat wa rabat. (7:154)

Among His signs, you see how desolate the earth is; yet whenever We send water down upon it, it stirs and sprouts. (Irving, 1985: 270)

The word (desolate) in English does not convey the Qur'anic concept of *khushuu'* (humility, piety, genuine love and fear of the Lord). Also in 31.

31   wa lammaa sakata 'an muusaa l-ghaDabu. (7:154)

When Moses' anger had subsided. (Irving, 1985: 84)

The metaphoric word *sakata*, which literally means 'to be silent', has been rendered into a non-metaphoric expression 'subside' (a metaphor in one language might not be the same in another), thus the rhetorical impact on the reader is not the same, neither is the rhetorical texture of the text. Similarly, the metaphor word *'ishta'ala* is rendered as a non-metaphor in 32 where *'ishta'ala* is given a rhetorically non-equivalent sense 'glisten', i.e. (to shine brightly).

32   Wa shta'ala r-ra'su shayban. (19:4)

And the hair of my head f\glistens with gray. (Ali, 1983: 767)

Oxymoron: This is a rhetorical relationship between two antonyms that occur next to each other.

33   sayaj'alu l-laahu ba'da 'usrin yusraa. (65:7)

After difficulty, God will soon grant relief. (Ali, 1983: 1565)

34   kutiba 'alayhi 'annahu man tawallahu fa'innahu yuDilluhu wa yahdiihi 'ila 'adhaabi s-sa'iir. (22:4)

About the (evil one) it is decreed that whoever turns to him for friend-ship, he will lead him astray, and he will guide him to the penalty of the fire. (Ali, 1983: 850)

The rhetorical relationship of the oxymoron between the words *'usrin* vs. *yusraa* (difficulty vs. relief) and *yuDilluhu* vs *yahdiihi* (lead astray vs. guide), in 33 and 34 respectively, is demolished and the oxymoron words are placed far apart from each other in the translation.

Tail-Head: Tail-Head occurs when a given statement is divided into two parts; the second part starts with a word similar to the last word of the first part as in 35 where the rhetorical relationship of Tail-Head, represented by *l-laahi wa l-laahu*, is lost in the target text.

35 qul yaa 'ahla l-kitaabi lima takfuruuna bi'aayaati l-laahi wa l-laahu shahiidun 'ala maa ta'maluun. (3:98)

Say: 'O followers of the earlier revelation! Why do you refuse to acknowledge the truth of God's message, when God is witness to all that you do?' (Asad, 1980: 82)

Cultural Voids

Cultural references are language / culture-specific. They can be exotic or emotive expressions and can either be transliterated or borrowed into the target language. Most cultural expressions are translation resistant such as *the Whip* and *P45* in English, or the French expression *au pair*. Some cultural expressions, however, can be linguistically tamed and naturalised into the target language, such as the Arabic expression *bukhuur*, which can be rendered into English as (air freshener), or the English expression (tooth-brush) which could have been naturalised as *miswaak* in Arabic. But these are instances of cultural transplantation. In Qur'anic discourse, we encounter a number of cultural expressions as in 36 and 37.

36 wa 'idhaa ra'aytahum tu'jibuka 'ajsaamuhum wa 'in yaquuluu tasma' liqawlihim ka'annahum khushubun musannada. (63:4)

When you look at them, their exteriors please you; and when they speak, you listen to their words. They are as worthless as hollow pieces of timber propped up, unable to stand on their own. (Ali, 1983: 1550)

37 wa 'idhaa laquukum qaaluu 'aamannaa wa 'idhaa khalaw 'aDDuu 'alaykumu l-'anaamila mina l-ghayzhi. (3:119)

When they meet you, they say: 'We believe', but when they are alone, they bite off the very tips of their fingers at you in their rage. (Ali, 1983: 153)

In 36, the expression *khushubun musannada* refers to the hypocrites. It is rendered through a periphrastic translation (worthless as hollow pieces of timber propped up, unable to stand on their own). Culturally, the Arabs used to put planks of timber against the wall at the back of their houses when they were not needed, and as such the planks of wood were useless most of the time. This expression reflects a metonymy for the person who is useless and worthless in the community. In 37, the cultural expression *'aDDuu l-'anaamila*, which is also provided with a periphrastic rendering 'to bite off the very tips of their fingers'. This is a cultural habit among some Arabs who express their anger or envy through biting the side of their index. To culturally transplant the two expressions into English, may suggest rendering them as *being useless as an old rag* and *to stamp their feet out of rage*, or *to gnash their teeth*, respectively.

Conclusion

Given the cultural and linguistic nature of sensitive discourse, in general, and the Qur'an, in particular, this chapter has tried to show, by no means exhaustively, some limits of translatability. The discussion has also shown that most Qur'an translations into English are source language orientated: they are marked by dogged adherence to source syntax, the use of archaic language and formal bias. Qur'anic discourse enjoys specific and unique features that are semantically orientated, and often create syntactic, lexical, stylistic, rhetorical and cultural voids in translation. As such, the features are Qur'an-bound and cannot be reproduced in an equivalent fashion in terms of structure, mystical effect on the reader, and intentionality. Without its features, the Qur'an will be reduced to an ordinary text.

Through communicative or literal translations, these unique features will be imposed on the English language readers. This linguistic marriage between the two linguistically and culturally incongruous languages can only lead to the deformation of the linguistic and rhetorical façade of the Qur'anic text and will create structural damage to its architectural beauty.

Bassnett (1991: 29) rightly warns that sameness cannot even exist between two target language versions of the text, let alone between the source language and the target language versions. Perfect equivalence, according to Casagrande (1954: 339), in the sense that the message evokes identical responses in the speakers of the two languages, is probably impossible to attain except perhaps in limited pragmatic messages. For the reasons discussed in this chapter, the translation of the Qur'an cannot be taken as a replacement of the Arabic source regardless of the accuracy and professionalism of the rendering. The Qur'anic message will always be inflicted with inaccuracies and skewing of information that can only be accounted for by the inclusion of informative exegetical footnotes. An English Qur'an is a translational impossibility.

Chapter 9

Translating Native Arabic Linguistic Terminology

SOLOMON I. SARA

Introduction

Translation is difficult and risky. A translator's objective is to transfer information from one language to another without betraying the former to accommodate the latter. The translator uses the tools available for the task. If the tools are plentiful and well established, then translation appears less demanding than if the endeavour demanded greater creativity.

The linguistic terminology in the Western tradition has been developed and well established. A look at the translation of Arabic linguistic works will show clearly that to go from the Arabic source to the Western target has been an easy undertaking for translators. After all, who would dare or care to change or challenge such firmly established universals like consonant and vowel, noun and verb, adjective and adverb? The issue here, however, is whether these terms are transferable across cultural and linguistic boundaries without residual distortion, or whether respect and fidelity to different linguistic traditions grant the linguistic sciences a larger perspective on the discipline beyond the traditionally established and partially fossilised terminological vocabularies.

Starting in the 8th century, the second century of Islam, Arab linguists demonstrated an uncommon interest in the analysis of Arabic and in the development of linguistics. In the process, they created a new science with an indigenous conceptual framework tailored to the exigencies of the language as they knew and spoke it. In this process of terminological creativity, they hewed a new path that avoided in both literal and figurative sense the corresponding terminological inventory most commonly used in other traditions. In translation of Arabic, the originality and the imagery of the Arab linguistic tradition have been recast into and subsumed under the vocabularies of the host languages. Translation has been faithful to its

107

Western roots and tools, but both the genius and the ethos of the Arab creators of linguistic terminology have been lost.

Preliminary Remarks

This chapter must, by necessity, be limited: it will touch only on basic terminologies used by both English and Arab linguists. The issue of concern is whether the corresponding terminological choices by both sets of linguists are comparable and reflect shared visions and shared intuitions about the same linguistic phenomena.

Besides the Arab tradition, there are two linguistic traditions that have established themselves and that can claim autonomy and independence. One is the Indian tradition, articulated by Panini in the 4th century BC, then revised by his commentators and followers. This tradition is well known to the English-speaking world. The second is the European or Western tradition, beginning with the Greek writers of logic, philosophy and science, and their reflections on language and its use. This tradition was adopted by the Latin writers in their treatises and has continued to our day. In this, also called the classical tradition, there have been many new developments in the study of language and linguistics: various schools have approached language and the study of language from different and often new perspectives.

Generally, one feels comfortable reading the treatises of the various schools despite their differences. Apart from certain novelties pertaining to individual schools, there is a remarkable consistency in the use of terminologies. A student of linguistics will come across a core inventory of linguistic terms such as vowel and consonant, noun and verb, subject and object, adjective and adverb, and the rest of the terminological repertoire developed over the centuries. It is concepts like these that define, for the most part, one's understanding of how a language is analysed and how it functions.

The richness of these linguistic vocabularies, their familiarity, and their pervasiveness both facilitate and hinder translation. This abundance of concepts makes it difficult to look at treatises on language from other traditions and with different perspectives. Translation is made both easy and difficult at the same time. It is made easy, because the richness makes understanding of language accessible: there is so much terminology that one is rarely at a loss to find the equivalents for what is expressed in another tradition. In the transmission of information, one sees one's own tradition and one's own frame of reference reflected in what is being said by others. Since the object of study is the same, language, then both the analysis and the synthesis must be shared irrespective of the idiom or the divergent terminological variance among the different traditions. Translating Arabic linguistic treatises into English, in this case, becomes easier since the apparatus of linguistic terminology, in English, is so large that it can capture whatever may be found in Arabic, and capture it fairly accurately.

The abundance of analytical tools in English and the availability of a well-developed and finely elaborated linguistic conceptual repertoire also make it difficult to see what is different or original in the other traditions, in this case, the Arabic tradition. One is not claiming that translating Arabic linguistic terminology into a current and well-established conceptual frame of reference is not valid. On the contrary, it is most welcome since it has been the vehicle to render the Arab tradition available to the wider world of linguistic thinking. However, analysis of Arabic using the established tools of another tradition conceals the creativity and originality brought to bear by Arab linguists on their own language and in their own way.

This applies particularly to the early stages of Arabic linguistic development, that is the 2nd century of the Islamic calendar, the 8th century of the common calendar. At this time two major figures, al-Farahidi (d. 786) as master, and Sibawaih (d. 793) as disciple, established the Arab linguistic tradition. The terminology discussed here will be taken from their works: *kitaab al-'ayn* (The Book of 'ayn), a dictionary, and *al-kitaab* (The Book), a grammar (cf. Sibawaih, 1881/1970, 1898; Sara, 1991, 1993). Their terminologies are, with few exceptions, still current in Arabic linguistic discourse (cf. Troupeau, 1976; Sara, 1996).

Linguistic Terminologies

Approaching this topic is perhaps most appropriately done by selecting specific terms and reflecting on them in both Arabic and English. Since English linguistic terminology has been inherited mostly from the Western classical tradition, and since the classical tradition has been alleged as one of the sources of Arabic linguistic tradition (cf. Versteegh, 1977), this chapter concentrates on the Western tradition as reflected in the shared concepts and vocabularies used both in English and Arabic, with comments on a selected number of such terms.

Lugha (dialect) and lahja (idiolect)

Language is a difficult concept to define and it is wiser to begin with dialect, which is easier to define since it is confined to a specific speech community. So, dialect is the 'language' of that group of speakers with all its attendant constraints and peculiarities when compared to the language of which it is a dialect. Linguists normally define dialect as a regionally or socially distinctive variety of language, with a particular lexis and grammar. Language, by contrast, is something more inclusive and more comprehensive, whose speakers are mythical beings of that abstract entity that pretends to prescind from its many actualities. Language can be defined as:

> Language is a purely human and non-instinctive method of communi-
> cating ideas, emotions, and desires by means of voluntarily produced
> symbols. (Sapir, 1921: 8)

> A language is a set (finite or infinite) of sentences each finite in length
> and constructed out of finite set of elements. (Chomsky, 1957: 13)

With these notions in mind, it is not easy to locate Arab linguists' definitions for language. Early Arab linguists tended to be illustrative in their approach to language, rather than definitional. There is a consistent use of the word *lugha* in Sibawaih, in contexts that make clear its intended meaning. When discussing language differences, he consistently refers to:

1. *lughatu banii tamiim*
   Language of Banii Tamiim
2. *lughatu ahli l-Hijaaz*
   Language of (the) people of Hidjaz
3. *lughatu bani 'asad*
   Language of banii 'asad

From these examples, he is not using language in the abstract sense but is closer to Western usage of 'dialect.' Even though one might be tempted to use *lugha* for language, it is not appropriate in these early treatises.

al-Farahidi (1980/85.3: 391) defines *lugha* as: *'ikhtilaafu l-kalaami fii ma'naa waaHid* (variance in speech with the same meaning). That is to say that *banii tamiim*, or *banii 'asad* and others vary their way of saying the same thing.

lahja: While *lahja* does not occur in Sibawayh, it comes up in al-Farahidi, which he defines variously as: *Tarafu l-lisaan* (edge of the tongue), *jarasu l-kalaam* (ring of speech), and as follows:

> *faSiiHu l-lahja wa hiya lughatuhu l-latii jubila 'alayhaa fa 'taadahaa wa
> nasha'a 'alayhaa.*
> Eloquent of *lahja*: it is his *lugha* of which he is made and grew upon and
> is accustomed to.

That is to say, the person's unique way of speaking. The term 'idiolect' can be used here, if one were generous with that term. So the current terms of language and dialect instead of dialect and idiolect respectively, miss their mark and veil what was clear to the early Arab linguists.

Haraka (motion) and sukuun (stillness)

Vowel versus consonant is the fundamental dichotomy in phonetics and phonology. Whatever these two terms mean, we know they refer to sounds like [i, a, u] and [p, t, k] respectively, and correspondingly to other sound segments. The terms vowel and consonant are borrowed Latin words and they are used only in linguistic discourse. Their meanings are obvious because of what they refer to, not because the concepts are well defined.

The Arab linguists drew neither on close etymological affinity nor on semantic relationship when they carried out their phonetic analyses. They perceived the sounds of Arabic in a totally different manner. They referred to the sounds of Arabic as *Huruuf* (letters), *Harf* (letter) (Lane, 1863.1: 549–50). The reference to letter is just one of its meanings and not the most fundamental. According to Lane, *Harf* has to do with deviation, hardship, leanness, fine edge, nib, and the extensions that come with these. *Hirfa* would be simply one's profession, not necessarily related to linguistics. Reference to the nib of a diagonally cut reed probably lead to the notion of letters produced with such an instrument. The Western concepts of vowel and consonant terms are far from what the Arabs had in mind.

sukuun: What is referred to as consonant here was referred to by the Arab linguists as *Harf saakin* (a still, quiescent letter) and the general term *sukuun* (stillness, quiescence). There is no hint that it is duplicating the basic meaning of the English/Latin term in the sense of its etymology *con+sonare*, to sound at the same time, along with a sonant. Consonant is a term that relates one type of segment to another, in this case, the sound that co-occurs with a sonant or a vowel. The Arabic notion is expressed in terms of no action, no motion and no activity to speak of. It gives it stillness. These letters become *con-sonants* only when they are in motion, set in motion by a *Haraka* (motion). Consonant is a Western term not Arab.

Haraka: What is referred to as vowel, the Arab linguists called *Haraka* (motion). This is a different image from the concept of vowel. Vowel is connected to voice, probably to the remote Latin word *vocalis* (something sonorous) which, in turn, sheds light on *con-sonant*. It is remote from the concept the Arabs used for this phenomenon. *Haraka* refers to the motion of the speech organs, not necessarily to the output of the motions. Translating *Haraka* and *sukuun* with vowel and consonant abandons the basic meanings of these terms and loses what originality the authors brought to this science. The dichotomy of *Haraka* and *sukuun* (motion, stillness) is a more elemental dichotomy than that of vowel and consonant.

Hayyiz (locale) and *makhraj* (exit)

Hayyiz involves the divisions of the vocal tract for articulation. *Hayyiz* (locale) for al-Farahidi (1980–1985) was a particular section of the oro-pharyngeal vocal tract where similar sounds with similar production were grouped. There were nine such locales which included areas of the oro-pharyngeal tract with reference to the upper and lower extensions in the cavity and to the whole cavity, and are located at: *Halq* (throat), *lahaa* (uvula), *shajr* (velum), *'asla* (apex), *niT'* (aveolum/palate), *lith-tha* (gingivae), *dhalaq* (laminae), *shafa* (lip), and the *jawf* (cavity). In addition to the upper divisions of the speech tract like *lahaa* (uvula) and *lith-tha* (gingivae), one finds *'asla* (apex) as one of the locales of speech production. So it is insufficient to refer to them as points of articulation.

For *makhraj* (exit) there is no real reflex in the English phonetic lexicon. Articulator and point of articulation are tools of the English phonetic lexicon to describe sound production. The active articulator approximates or makes contact with the point of articulation and in the process a sound is produced. The Arab linguists' conception of *makhraj* is a different image. It is a three dimensional visualisation of articulation where the vocal tract assumes specific shapes for the different *Huruuf* (letters) of the language. It is that tunnel, formation at a particular narrow constriction at the specified locale that determines which letter is being formed and articulated, the narrowing of the speech channel that creates a *makhraj*. Translating *makhraj* with (point of articulation) mis-translates the term and loses both the three dimensional image and the intent that the Arabic term captures.

Shadiid (tight) and *rakhw* (loose)

The term *shadiid* has been translated as (stop), in the sense of a blockage. But it is a stop according to another tradition of linguistics. In harmony with the basic understanding of the vocal tract as a tube, constrictions of any kind along the length of this tube are called (exits). With the three dimensional image in mind, in total closure of a flexible, tube-like structure, *tight* is the appropriate term and not *stop*.

The term *rakhw* has been translated as 'fricative'. Again, it is fricative according to a different tradition in the sense of the sound produced. In the tube-like vocal tract any partial constriction, as opposed to a total constriction, would be termed *rakhw*, that is a loose noose.

In the Arab tradition, the two concepts have a different view on what takes place in the production of sounds like [t] and [s] and [k] or [x]. They capture the dynamic nature of the action that takes place in producing sounds like [k] or [x]. It is clear these terms were chosen advisedly to accord with the other two notions of *Hayyiz* and *makhraj*. They specify the type of exit that is produced. It was an attempt to be harmonious with the primary division of the vocal tract into locales and exits. Tight and loose preserve the insights of those who selected the terms to stand for those concepts.

Majhuur (loud) and *mahmuus* (muted)

The term *majhuur* has been translated as 'voiced.' Sounds like [d] and [z] are indeed captured by the description of voice as opposed to voiceless for [t] and [s], for example. However convenient, this term does not translate *majhuur*. There is, first of all, a technical issue to be resolved. The current understanding of 'voice' refers to the actions of the larynx, and more specifically to the vibrations of the vocal chords. The 8th century Arab linguists had no idea of the function of the larynx. The word larynx is not mentioned in their description of the production of sounds. Attribution of the concept of voice to this term, according to Western understanding, is gratuitous and inaccurate. The term is to be understood as it would be in ordinary discourse: the sounds may be loud and more audible or less so, that is, more muted. According to lexical evidence, *majhuur*, with reference to sound, was simply a loud sound.

The term *mahmuus* is translated by 'voiceless'. The same reasoning applies here as to *majhuur*. Since the functions of the larynx were unknown to early linguists, attributions to the functions of the larynx are inappropriate, and 'voiceless' for all its convenience and familiarity is neither accurate nor acceptable. The early Arab linguists had a clear idea what they meant by the term: 'it is rather whispered in the mouth like a secret'.

'Ism (name) and *fi'l* (act)

The universal translation of these two terms is 'noun' and 'verb'. There should be no objection to these, in general, except that Arabic is precise in its terms. One is the common word for a *name*, and the other is the common word for an *act* – that is, any name and any act. Thus they are generic. Another objection to noun and verb is that these terms are exclusively linguistic terms and not part of general discourse, while the Arabic terms are indeed part of general discourse. Derivations of noun revert to the Latin stem, for example 'nominal'. The Arabic clearly and naturally captures this in *'ism* (name) and *'ismii* (nominal). Verbal does not necessarily imply action, so its derivations shift the semantic burden to another domain, to the domain of words in general. Using 'name' and 'act' represents a clearer and a less ambiguous choice for the translation of the Arabic terms.

Dharf zamaan (envelope of time) *dharf makaan* (envelope of place)

These are translated often as 'adverb of time' and 'adverb of place,' which they are. The only point to be made is that the images of the Arabic choices provide explicit ideas of enclosures, of something with limits and edges to it, whether of time or place, which the English terms do not do. Without putting too fine a point on it, *ad-verbum* is more closely related to other words than the concept itself indicates. The choices of 'envelope of time' and 'envelope of place', respectively capture the Arabic pair accurately. The two English terms, like some of the others, occur only in linguistic discourse.

Sifah (descriptive)

The translation for this term is invariably 'adjective'. The choice of a common word in Arabic makes it more accessible to the user of the language. Meaning is clear by use. Adjective, with all its pervasiveness in linguistic descriptions, is limited to linguistic discourse about language. It has no clear image associated with it. *Aa-jacere*, like *ad-verbum*, only hints that it is a form that is thrown in with some other forms of words. It is a sequential or co-occurrence reference, while the Arabic choice of *Sifah* (descriptive, description) is a meaningful term.

'Imaala (inclination)

Classical Arabic has three *Harakaat* (motions, vowels). A perfect triangle. When one begins manipulating these *Harakaat*, one finds that the image of the relationship of the *Harakaat*, in the minds of the Arab linguists, was not that of a triangle. It is awkward to discuss *'imaala* with its attendant processes by using the image of a triangle. It appears that the more appropriate image that captures the relationship among the *Harakaat* of Arabic is that of a tee T formation. This makes the process of *'imaala* easier to explain. The relationships of the *Harakaat* is shown in the Figure 1.

The *'imaala* process was the pronunciation of *alif* [A] as a front or back sound. Its motion towards the *yaa'* [j], its pronunciation as an [e], as happens in so many modern Arabic dialects, was one form of *'imaala*, and

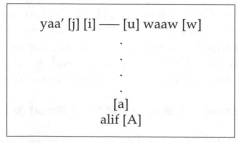

Figure 1

its motion towards the *waaw* [w] in the process of *tafkhiim* (emphasis) was another form of *'imaala*. This brings up the issue of the translation of the term. Umlauting is appropriate if one were to confine oneself to the familiar term. In *'imaala*, the *alif* [A] shifts both to the right and to the left, so the more appropriate translation of the concept is inclination or one of its synonyms. That is, the bar or the stem of the T, that indicates the [A], leans towards [j] to the left, or towards [w], to the right, to attain the proper sound production.

Conclusion

In the history of linguistics, one keeps in mind what Itkonen (1991: 125) said:

> ... the Western linguistic theory has been almost completely unaware of the insights that the Arab linguists have contributed to the field. This is owing to the fact that until recently even the Western experts, hampered by some sort of 'Indo-European' bias, have been unable to assess Arab linguistics at its true value.

Indeed, some writers of the history of linguistics ignore the Arab contribution completely (Auroux, 1989: 13–37).

The discussion in this chapter of a selection of technical linguistic terms used by the early Arab linguists is a small sample of terms that pose problem in translating Arabic linguistic terms into English. A faithful translation needs to reflect the linguistic thinking of the linguists in question. Only in faithfully and accurately transmitting their thoughts will one be able to assess their contributions to the study of Arabic in particular and to linguistic thinking in general. Early Arab linguists concentrated their efforts almost exclusively on analysis of Arabic, but in the process they managed to create a science that reflected the nature of Arabic, its components, its constructions and its attendant difficulties.

These early linguists had only their own language to forge a metalanguage to discuss it. From the few examples mentioned above and from the hundreds of others in their treatises, one finds nothing but common Arabic words that have been used to express new and discipline-specific extensions, in addition to their common meanings. There is no trace of any borrowed imagery or conceptual frame of reference used as a template for this new discipline. If they had at their disposal Indian, Greek, Latin, or any other source of linguistic terminology, they showed poor ability in translating them into their language. It seems fair to say that they had no such ready-made system, which they could adapt to their specific needs. They were their own masters of their own language. Their output in this area of linguistics is the result of their efforts, their deliberations and their discussions in the successful creation of a new science of linguistics with an Arabic base.

English linguistic terminology is, for the most part, a derivative vocabulary inherited from the classical tradition and reserved for linguistics. It is a vocabulary that has not penetrated into general discourse but has been confined to specific use in technical linguistic discussions. This is different from Arabic, whose technical linguistic terminology grew out of its own vocabulary and has maintained its dual function, common and technical. Certainly, there are degrees of fidelity in translating one set of concepts into another. In the process of moving from Arabic to English, there is variance in translation. Some of the terms are totally different in the two traditions (*Haraka, sukuun*). Others are a question of usage at the time, while others are a question of conceptual precision.

Finally, the argument here is not intended to imply that most Arabic technical linguistic terminology has been mis-translated. That would be false. The purpose has been to point out that the universality and the ready availability of some of the basic concepts of linguistics that define one's approach to language analysis pose a challenge to the translator. The translator is tempted to opt for the familiar and the available rather than introduce the novel and the unfamiliar into the tradition. Accurate translation of the new concepts provides the information needed to understand the Arab tradition. Arabic linguistic concepts are part of the rich tradition that was the result of a robust linguistic movement among the Arabs. It is in the totality of these unfamiliar and novel terms that the originality of the Arab linguists is clearly demonstrated.

Chapter 10

Towards an Economy and Poetics of Translation from and into Arabic[1]

RICHARD JACQUEMOND
Translated from French by Philip Tomlinson

Introduction

As a translator of contemporary Egyptian works into French and as an organiser of an aid programme for translation of French works into Arabic and their publication in Egypt, I have frequently had cause to observe that, contrary to appearances, what I used to refer to in both directions as translation related in fact to quite different practices depending on whether it was into French or Arabic. Similarly, in a more general way, I found that the work I was doing had neither the same meaning nor the same implications depending on whether it was intended for the French or the Egyptian cultures. Endeavouring to locate answers to my questions in the literature on translation, I was more often than not disappointed. Linguistic theories, teaching manuals, the doxological writings of translators were all unhelpful to the sense I had that the crux of the matter lay elsewhere, in the history of the relations between the Arab and French cultures.

Much has been said and written about translation from and into Arabic in the modern era, in linguistic or literary studies or in the historiography – orientalist and native – of Arab culture (the task of listing and gathering together this body of writing is surely one which the Toledo School of Translators will have to undertake). However, as far as I am aware, we do not have at our disposal a study explicitly on the traffic of translation between Arabic and the main European languages construed both theoretically and historically. For a number of years through contributions such as this, I have personally been making attempts to provide one, without being able to devote myself entirely to it (see Jacquemond, 1992, 1993). This last point may be taken as an excuse for anything hypothetical or even intuitive about any of the proposals advanced here, my chapter aiming primarily to

117

put forward research yet to be undertaken rather than conclusions of an already completed project.

Until very recently, research in translation was very much a matter of breaking new scientific ground. It is only since the 1970s, particularly with the first publications of what is now commonly called the polysystem school, Even-Zohar and Gideon Toury in Tel-Aviv, and Lambert in Louvain (cf. Lambert, 1989), that translation began to be thought of as a total sociolinguistic and cultural phenomenon. Yet, despite the contributions of this school, it seems to me that it lacks a sociological theory. I shall borrow the sociology required from Bourdieu, whose theory of fields is, I think, the most productive analytical tool for analysis of the market in symbolic goods (Bourdieu, 1992).[2] Given these premises, my starting point is to see how the problem of translation is posed in each of the cultures concerned.

The Status of Translation within Modern Arab and French Cultures

The absence in Bourdieu's work on literature of any reference to translation must not prevent us from attempting to adapt his theory to it, and first by pointing out that this 'hole' in Bourdieu's analysis is connected to his construction of the cultural field as closed and self-sufficient. If he can construct it in this way, it is only because he is speaking from within what Lambert calls a stable culture or a culture which tends to integrate imported texts by imposing its own conventions on them. In this we can trace the model Berman calls ethnocentric translation, for which he formulates two axioms:

> We ought to translate the foreign work so that we do not 'feel' the translation, we ought to translate in a way that gives the impression that this is what the author would have written if he had written in the language of the translation. (1985: 53)

In a stable culture, translation tends to be invisible, since it is not seen as giving rise to any issues of culture and is pushed beyond the fringes of the cultural field (Venuti, 1995). Such was the situation for a long time in French culture, and *a contrario*, the renewed interest in translation, which we see in France whether in terms of theory or of practice (in teaching, public policies, etc.) arises out of recent recognition of the loss of French culture's dominant position.

The situation is obviously very different in modern Arab culture. Here, translation very quickly became an essential commonplace of the Arab renaissance, the *nahDa*; it is highly pertinent that Tahtawi, an emblematic figure of the *nahDa*, was primarily a translator. Commanded by the Khedivs, Tahtawi translated and had translated a number of pragmatic texts (school and university textbooks between 1830 and 1840, legal codes in the 1870s), and made a decisive contribution to the first modernisation of the Arabic language. From that time onwards, language and translation have long been central issues in Arab culture. As the language of a dominated culture, Arabic is condemned to assimilate and translate a material and symbolic universe, in the production of which its speakers take no part.

In this sense, the history of Arab culture, from Tahtawi to the present, could be written through the prism of translation. It would show, for example, that in the 19th century, and into the first and second decades of the 20th century, literary translation ran along clearly different lines from pragmatic translation. Whereas the former began later and for a long time functioned 'ethnocentrically' early on, the latter transformed Arabic lexis and style. The difference corresponds fully with the reformist project preceding colonisation, namely with the idea of bridging the 'material' gulf with Europe, whilst making no 'spiritual', that is moral and aesthetic, concessions. The colonial period, which saw the influence of European languages becoming stronger everywhere, was a period when in all spheres there was little translation. Arab culture then tended to divide into two sub-cultures, which were to varying degrees self-contained: a hermetically sealed monolingual sub-culture, and an 'evolved' sub-culture, as it was then described, with access to the culture of the coloniser present in the text.

A contrario, when countries became politically independent, there were many efforts to end the schizophrenia through the promotion of Arabicisation, and thus translation. As in the 19th century, public policy support for translation began to flourish once more; in Egypt the *alf kituub*, or 1000 book project launched in 1955 by Taha Hussein; in Lebanon the Lebanese Commission for the translation of great works, in Iraq, Syria, etc. The Maghreb later followed suit. This 'developmentalist' conception of translation was also seen in the legal status of the translated work. The 1954 Egyptian law on copyright (article 8) limits protection of foreign works translated into Arabic to five years from the date of publication of the original, thus overriding the normal limit of fifty years after the death of the author. Similar measures can be found in the statutes of other Arab states and are more widespread in those of Third World countries where the international law on intellectual property, which gives the same protection to original and translated texts, is an impediment to the intellectual development of their peoples. Even today, and despite the fact that the majority of Arab states are signatories to one or other international copyright convention (the Paris or the Berne conventions), Arab culture as a whole continues to view foreign intellectual production as some kind of 'commonwealth of mankind', on which anyone and everyone has the right to draw.

In this way, translation is a very different issue, depending on whether it is viewed from Paris or Cairo. It will now be shown that the dominant factor in the way French culture relates to Arab culture is the marginalisation of translation through 'orientalism', whereas in the Arab world the overwhelming fact is the omnipresence of translation and the marginalisation of 'occidentalism'; in other words, of knowledge of the West produced by and for Arab culture.

Translation from Arabic and the Orientalist Field

In the French book market, translation almost invariably makes up some 15 to 20% of publications per annum. Within this number, the proportion of translation from Arabic is insignificant: some 10 to 30 titles, very probably less than 1% of all published translations! Even more interestingly, the proportion is just as marginal when compared with the number of titles published in French and related in some way to the Arab world, which amount to several hundreds per year (cf. Barret-Ducrocq, 1992).[3]

This epitomises the quasi-monopoly over the representation of the Arab world in modern French culture held by what I propose to call the *orientalist field*. The term should be understood not in the 'academic' sense of the scientific investigation of the Arab world or the Orient, but in the sociological sense of all those – individuals and institutions – that, in the first instance for the French market, produce and disseminate discourse about the Arab world. I use the qualifier orientalist with no derogatory connotations, but simply to underline an essential reality: in France, representation of the Arab world in mediated and mediatised. Irrespective of nationality, origin or residence, he who produces a work whose subject is the Arab world, but which in the first instance is produced for and distributed to, the French market, belongs to the orientalist field.

This approach has several advantages. For example, it enables us to explain how orientalist representations of the colonial period are still reproduced and developed today by different agents. The orientalist painters and other romantic travellers have been succeeded by tourists, journalists, photographers, etc., but the stereotypes have barely changed. This is in spite of a huge transformation in the sociology of those who belong to the French orientalist field, which has become heavily populated by intellectual producers from the Arab world (writers, scientists, artists and others). Of course, these Arab producers are still obliged to negotiate their position in relation to the paradigms of traditional orientalist representation, and to renew their allegiance to the fundamental values of French culture, as we see every time there is a new political or ideological conflict between France (or Europe, or the West) and the Arab and/or Islamic world. However, it is undeniable that they help fashion French representation of the Arab world, and they do so in two areas: at the heart of the orientalist field, within what Bourdieu calls the sub-field of restricted production (production aimed at other producers), and at its boundaries, where some producers deliberately target several constituencies, operating simultaneously in both French and Arab markets.

However, in either case, the market is occupied by the French orientalist field, leaving only a tiny place for the direct import of Arab works and for translation, and, into the bargain, filtering them in terms of its own mindset. Quantitatively marginalised, translation from Arabic is also massively determined, in its economy and poetics, by the orientalist field.

Arabic-French Translation is Orientalising Translation

Against the prevailing mode of translation in France, which aims to gallicise and naturalise, translation from Arabic has long been a factor in embedding in the mind of the francophone reader the image of a culture that is different, radically other. It has done so via different modes, but their cumulative effects have increased the sense of otherness: philological translation used in the academic sub-field, and exoticising translation which developed in the orientalist field aiming at a broad audience.

Berman reminds us that philological translation started in the 19th century as a reaction to the tradition of free translation, the *belles infidèles* of the classical era. Philology established and fixed ancient texts (Greek, Roman, Oriental) and produced exact translations with no literary ambitions, aiming 'simply to restore the meaning of the texts' (Berman, 1985). The priority was to reproduce the original as closely as possible, and then to overload it with critical apparatus, along the lines of manuscript editing. Orientalism exhumes the *turaath* (tradition) but in order better to mummify it, in that it makes the works accessible to us, but in unreadable translations, which at the same time widens the distance between them and us. It enshrines in the target language the image of a 'complicated Orient', to use de Gaulle's expression, and in doing so, not only reinforces that very stereotype, but also confirms the orientalist's status as the expert and as the indispensable mediator. An archetypal figure of this tradition, and of the degree of appropriation of Arab texts it is capable of, is the translation by

Régis Blachère of the Qur'an with its chronological reclassification of the *Suras*.

At the same time, as a result of the fashion for travel to the Orient, the 19th century also witnessed a rapid growth of *exoticising* translations. We can gauge the distance between 'gallicising translation', which dominates classical French culture, and exoticising translation through the comparison of two well known French translations of the *Thousand and One Nights*: Galland's early 18th-century version, which is generally faithful to the *belles infidèles* model, and Mardrus' late 19th-century translation, which is a model of exoticising translation, in which 'the translator 'puts in bits of his own' in order to 'make it more real' by stressing the vernacular, a stereotyped image of which provides his starting point' (Berman, 1985: 79). The gap between the two translations is not just to do with the personalities of the translators, but faithfully reflects the shift in the French outlook on Arab culture in the two centuries separating them.

The orientalising tendencies in Arabic-French translation were for a long time set to focus exclusively on ancient texts, orientalism having established the idea that Arab culture had produced its best centuries ago, and that it would no longer produce anything worth exporting. It was not until the 1930s and 1940s that modern Arab works were translated, initially in penny numbers, though increasingly for the past 20 years or so. Even then, works with a traditional stamp are of course not broached, rather those closest to our aesthetics and values, by the most 'acculturated' authors. We do not translate Muwaylihi's *Hadiith 'isa bnu Hisham*, but works such as *Un Substitut de campagne en Egypte* (English trans. *Maze of Justice: Diary of a Country Prosecutor*) by Tawfiq al-Hakim (published in Arabic in 1937 and in French translation the following year), *Le Livre des jours* (English trans. *The Steam of Days*) by Taha Hussein (published in Arabic in 1929 and in French in 1947), in other words, writers educated in France, and of all their works only those marked by the contrast between, on the one hand, their modernist European ideals and values, and, on the other, their description of a 'backward' native society. In this respect, we ought to reread André Gide's preface to the translation of *Le Livre des jours*, which is all about binary oppositions between East and West, darkness and light, progress and backwardness, etc.

So, in its very economy, translation from Arabic confirms the idea prevailing in France that not only is Arab culture dead, but that its modern productions are worthless, unless they stem from 'civilised' natives, who have assimilated our forms and values, and thus confirm from within Arab culture itself the representation of a radical separation between tradition and modernity, backwardness and progress, etc. The result is a huge gulf between the reception of such works in their source culture and in the culture of translation. If authors willingly widen the contrast between, on the one hand, their modern ideals and values, and, on the other, the description of a traditional 'backward' society, it is because in the eyes of the Arab reader they seek better to communicate a social critique and a demand for modernisation. However, the French reader receives these texts as ethnographic documents (_Un Substitut de campagne_ was republished by Plon in the _Terre Humaine_ (_Human Earth_) series which specialises in this type of literature), useful for finding out about the 'customs of the country' (Tomiche, 1978). And the 'documents' are all the better received since they confirm at the same time the otherness of the other culture (backward, authoritarian . . .) and the representation French culture bestows on itself (modern, democratic . . .) – confirmation all the more gratifying since it stems from the other. It is as if translation were condemned to oscillate between the two antagonistic, yet complementary, poles of _exoticisation_ and _naturalisation_.

A good example of the implicit meaning of this oscillation is Naguib Mahfouz, the first and only contemporary Arab writer to this day to have been translated and read on a relatively wide scale. A precise analysis of the translation and reception of Mahfouz in France (and, no doubt, elsewhere) would show that his success derives less from the facile dialectic of the 'particular and the universal', copiously referred to by Arab and non-Arab critics following the award of the Nobel Prize in 1988, than from the creation of work which lends itself both to an exoticising and to a naturalising reception: solidly realistic novels, which conform to the Western canons of the novel and which give the reader his money's worth, in that they give him an overall vision of the 'customs of the country'. However, not all Mahfouz's works come under such a broad definition and those furthest from it (novellas written after 1967, for example) are never chosen for translation. Moreover, while Mahfouz is read in Egypt as the _historian_ of contemporary Egypt (Mehrez, 1994), he is introduced abroad as the ethnographer of the 'ordinary people of Cairo', fixed, like an orientalist painting, in the 'highly colourful' image painted by their 'chronicler' – frequent expressions in French newspaper reviews.

Whilst the integration of such literature into the ordinary publishing market will have put the exoticising poetics of Arabic-French translation (in its philological and over-Arabicising variants) clearly on the back foot, everything shows that in terms of what I call the economy of these translations (selection of works for translation, publishers' policies on presentation and distribution of this type of literature, critical and public reception) almost everything continues to operate according to what one might call, paraphrasing Bourdieu, the rules of orientalist art.

Economy and Poetics of Contemporary Arabic Translation

In the absence of statistics and even remotely systematic bibliographies, precise figures on the share of translated books in the Arab market cannot be given. At least it can be noted that the share is much smaller than it ought to be in view of the position of Arab culture in global trends in production and traffic of the written word. If translated books make up barely 5% of Anglo-Saxon publications (a powerfully dominant and very closed culture), 15 to 20% of French or German publications (averagely dominant and relatively open cultures), and upwards of 40 to 50% of publications in countries whose languages carry little or no weight in international exchanges, the Arab market might be expected to be somewhere between the last two cases. However, all indications point to the fact that translation at best represents 10 to 15% of published titles. Why? First, Arabicisation of the market is not yet complete. In some countries (the Maghreb) and in some publishing sectors (medicine and exact sciences), texts in the foreign language still take up a large place. Secondly, part of foreign intellectual production passes into Arabic via translators who do not describe themselves as such: with university textbooks, it is known that texts by Arab writers frequently contain varying amounts of translation. Whatever the extent of such factors (and they are hard to quantify), the fact remains that the Arab market is relatively open to foreign publications.

To look now at the general economy governing such translations, it would seem that the first thing to note is that, for translation into Arabic, priority is given to texts about the Arab world written in foreign languages. I say 'seem', since the priority is not apparent in bibliographies, which classify books according to their discipline (literature, human sciences, etc.) and not according to their subject matter; it is nonetheless obvious to any observer of the Arab book market. From the Arabian Gulf to the Atlantic Ocean across the Nile Valley, each country translates first those orientalist texts (as defined above), which are about itself. Throughout the modern era, it is in this type of literature – and particularly among authors who are seen as sympathisers with the Arab or Islamic cause, such as Gustave Le Bon yesterday and Roger Garaudy today – that the best-sellers of translation into Arabic will be found. This is currently advantageous to Arab authors writing in French, but one may wonder whether in these cases it is really a matter of translation into Arabic, and whether it is rather a 'return to the original', as is suggested by the title of the series '*awdatu n-naS*, The Return of the Text (jointly published by Le Seuil and the Tunisian publisher Cérès), which, in the 1980s, published a sequence of Arabic translations of Maghrebi texts written in French. It is an area which in other respects raises a number of exciting issues for the poetics of translation, whether for those who bring 'that bi-language', as Abdelkébir Khatibi calls it, 'back to Arabic' or for those who translate such works into other languages (see Mehrez, 1992).

However, if one sets aside the particular case of the 'return' of orientalist production to its source culture, the share of translation in the Arab book market is even more minimal than stated. In looking at how it is made up, the first thing to note is the suffocating dominance of two source languages, English and French, each with its zone of influence which maps very precisely, even today, onto former colonial partitions: French in Lebanon, Syria and the Maghreb, English in Iraq, Jordan and the Arabian Peninsula. Egypt is a special case, in that the British occupation, from 1882, did not stop the continuation of a certain French influence. Throughout the Arab world, other languages are marginalised.

An attempt will now be made to outline the general features of the economy and poetics of French-Arabic translation. As far as selection of texts for translation is concerned, the main factor, compared to the 1950s and 1960s, is the decline of literature and the rise of human sciences. However, the trend is not specific to translation into Arabic, since recent French literature has generally travelled less well than the human sciences, though it is more noticeable in Arab territories than in other language areas. If we were to draw up a current list of available foreign literature in Arabic translation (the total number of continually republished titles), we would be surprised at how small it is, unless it were to include translations which are republished as original works owing to the fame of their authors, as in the case of the translations of Manfaluti and, in a very different style, of Taha Hussein.

Though, in its present economy, translation into Arabic frequently reflects a return to a certain ethnocentrism, a distancing from the foreign, the opposite evolution would be observed in its poetics. Arabicisation (*ta'riib*), a naturalising mode of translation given elevated rank by the great author-translators of the 1940s and 1950s, seems to have been succeeded by a more servile, more literal mode of translation, which reveals the source language in the lexis and syntax of the Arabic. This is connected to the general evolution of the language, which today seems more than ever permeable to foreign influences. On top of this, the progressive blurring of the boundaries between written languages and spoken varieties, which are by nature more prone to accommodate borrowings and calques, merely highlights the phenomenon. It is also connected to the decline in the material and symbolic status of the Arab translator, and more generally to the limited professionalism of Arab publishing, which too often leads to the publication of incomprehensible texts for the *arabophone* reader, unless he is bilingual and capable of mentally retranslating the Arab text he is reading into the original. These days, we often hear it said that translation into Arabic has become so servile that the average Arab reader realises from the first page whether he has in front of him a translation or a text written in Arabic. This kind of assessment, which one probably comes across nowadays in all 'peripheral' cultures, says a lot about the pressures to which the Arabic language is presently subjected. But we should not underestimate the capacity of cultures to naturalise foreign contributions, sometimes extremely rapidly – similar to the occurrence of a fashion.

Contradictory Values of Naturalisation and Exoticisation

'Translatologists', as they are now called, usually distinguish between two modes of translation as old as translation itself, one favouring the target language and the other the source language. I hope to have shown here that these two modes are not invested with absolute values and meanings, but that, on the contrary, their stylistic modalities and the respective symbolic and ideological meanings with which they are charged are radically different depending on whether they occur in a linguistically and culturally dominant area, or in a linguistically and culturally dominated area. The ethnocentrism of translation into French, the ideal of which is invisibility of translation and translator, has nothing to do with the 'cannibalistic' ethnocentrism of translation into Arabic, which, on the contrary, makes the author disappear behind the translator. Conversely, the over-Arabicisation, whether philological or exoticising, of translation into French has nothing to do with the servile and literal over-gallicising of translation into Arabic.

Taking these ideas further, one would say that all this research into the comparative economy and poetics of translation only makes sense if it helps to bring out the ethical basis of the act of translating. And, if this ethical basis is unique – the translator is contributing to a less alienating knowledge of the Other, both for the latter and for himself – it posits the implementation of opposite translation strategies whenever the cultures concerned are as manifestly unequal as Arab and French cultures are today. On the Arabic side, we need more 'cultural cannibalism', a return to ethnocentric and Arabicising translation. On the French side, on the other hand, we need to develop new modes of translation that break with the gallicisation/exoticisation alternation. It is a difficult way forward, but it is one along which the translator has been preceded by Arab authors writing in French, who, when they do not yield to the temptations of self-orientalisation, have developed a whole strategy for subverting language and writing in order to make their difference heard.[4]

Notes

1. The French version of this article, 'Pour un Économie et une Poétique de la Traduction de et vers l'Arabe', appeared in Miguel Hernando de Larramendi and Gonzalo Ferández Parrilla (eds) *Pensamiento y circulación de las ideas en el Mediterráneo: el papel de la traducción*. Toledo: Universidad de Castilla-La Mancha (1997).

2. In the following extract P. Bourdieu clearly shows, in my view, the heuristic potential of the notion of field: 'La notion de champ permet de dépasser l'opposition entre lecture interne et analyse externe sans rien perdre des acquis et des exigences de ces deux approches, traditionnellement perçues comme inconciliables. Conservant ce qui est inscrit dans la notion d'intertextualité, c'est-à-dire le fait que l'espace des oeuvres se présente àchaque moment comme un champ de positions qui ne peuvent être comprises que relationnellement, en tant que systèmes d'écarts différentiels, on peut poser l'hypothèse (confirmée par l'analyse empirique) d'une homologie entre l'espace des oeuvres défini dans leur contenu proprement symbolique, et en particulier dans leur *forme*, et l'espace des positions dans le champ de production (...); en effet, du fait du jeu des homologies entre le champ littéraire et le champ du pouvoir ou le champ social dans son ensemble, la plupart des stratégies littéraires sont surdéterminées et nombre des 'choix' sont des *coups doubles*, à la fois esthétiques et politiques, internes et externes'. (1992: 288-9)

3. A survey by the Institut du Monde Arabe on French publishing output in 1986 (in *Le Monde Arabe dans la vie intellectuelle et culturelle en France*, Colloque, 18-20 Janvier 1988, Institut du Monde Arabe, 1989), and a study carried out at the behest of the Centre national des lettres et de la Direction du Livre et de la Lecture, ministère français de la Culture (National Centre for Literature and for the Control of Books and Reading, French Ministry of Culture); see Fr. Barret-Ducrocq (1992).

4. 'L'écriture française nous 'livre' à l'autre, mais on se décentrage incessant de la phrase et du langage, de maniè que l'autre se perde comme dans les ruelles de la casbah' (Abdelwahab Meddeb, quoted in Jean Déjeux (1982) *Situation de la littérature maghrébine de langue française* (pp. 103-4). Algiers: OPU.

Bibliography

Adab, B.J. (1996) *Annotated Texts for Translation: English-French*. Clevedon: Multilingual Matters.

Ahmad, A. (1992) *In Theory: Classes, Nations, Literatures*. London: Verso.

Ali, A.Y. (1983) *The Holy Qur'an: Text, Translation and Commentary*. Maryland: Amana Corp.

Ali, M.J. (1981) *Scheherzade in England: A Study of Nineteenth-Century English Criticism of the Arabian Nights*. Washington, DC: Three Continents Press.

Ambjörsson, R. (1999) Att odla mänsklighet. *Dagens Nyheter* (Swedish daily) 7 January.

Amit-Kochavi, H. (1996) Israeli Arabic literature in Hebrew translation: Initiation, dissemination and reception. *The Translator* 2:1, 27–44.

Amit-Kochavi, H. (2000) Hebrew translations of Palestinian literature – from total denial to partial recognition. *TTR* XIII (1), 53–80

Arberry, A.J. (1980) *The Koran Interpreted*. Oxford: Oxford University Press.

Asad, M. (1980) *The Message of the Qur'an*. Gibraltar: Dar al-Andalus.

Asad, T. (1995) A comment on translation, critique, and subversion. In A. Dingwaney and C. Maier (eds) *Between Languages and Cultures* (pp. 325–32). Pittsburgh: University of Pittsburgh Press.

Asaf, O. (1984) An encounter that hasn't taken place – on Arabic music and Western music. *Iton 77*, 27–57 (in Hebrew).

Ashcroft, B., Griffiths, G. and Tiffin, H. (2000) *Post-Colonial Studies. The Key Concepts*. London and New York: Routledge.

Auroux, S. (1989) *Histoire des idées linguistique, Tome I: la naissance des métalangues en Orient et en Occident*. Liège-Bruxelles: Mardaga.

Bahat, A. (1972) We're in the east while our hearts are in the distant west. *Ofeg 2*, 183–92 (in Hebrew).

Bakhtin, M. (1994) *The Dialogic Imagination: Four Essays*. Austin: University of Texas Press.

Ballas, S. (1970) *Arabic Literature under the Shadow of War*. Tel Aviv: Am Oved Publishing House (in Hebrew).

Barret-Ducrocq, Fr. (ed.) (1992) *Traduire l'Europe*. Paris: Payot.

Bassnett, S. (1991) *Translation Studies*. London: Routledge.

Bassnett, S. (1998a) Translating across cultures. In S. Hunston (ed.) *Language at Work* [British Studies in Applied Linguistics 13] (pp. 72–85). Clevedon: Multilingual Matters.

Bassnett, S. (1998b) Translating the seed: Poetry and translation. In S. Bassnett and A. Lefevere *Constructing Cultures* (pp. 57–75). Clevedon: Multilingual Matters.

Bauman, R. (1977) *Verbal Art as Performance*. Rowley, MA: Newbury House.

Bauman, Z. (1996) From pilgrim to tourist – or a short history of identity. In S. Hall and P. du Gay (eds) *Questions of Cultural Identity* (pp. 18–36). London: Sage Publications.

Beekman, J. and Callow, J. (1974) *Translating the Word of God.* Zondervan: Grand Rapids, Michigan.

Bell, R.T. (1991) *Translation and Translating: Theory and Practice.* London: Longman.

Benjamin, W. (1969) *Illuminations.* New York: Schoken Books.

Ben-Yehuda, E. (1940/1960) *A Complete Dictionary of Ancient and Modern Hebrew.* New York and London: Thomas Yoseloff.

Berman, A. (1985) La traduction et la lettre ou L'auberge du lointain, *Les tours de Babel*, TER.

Berque, J. (1978) *Cultural Expression in Arab Society Today.* Austin: University of Texas Press. Originally published as *Langages arabes du présent* (1974). Paris: éditions Gallimard.

Berque, J. (1995) *Egypt: Imperialism and Revolution.* Furulund: Alhambra. Originally published as *L'Égypte: imperialisme et révolution* (1967), Paris.

Bhabha, H. (1994) *The Location of Culture.* London and New York: Routledge.

Bjärvall, K. (1998) Översättningar kräver en varsam hand. *Metro* (Swedish daily), 19 August.

Bourdieu, P. (1991) *Language and Symbolic Power.* Cambridge: Polity Press.

Bourdieu. P. (1992) *Les régles de l'art, Genèse et structure du champ littéraire.* Paris: Le Seuil.

Bourdieu, P. (1993) *The Field of Cultural Production.* Cambridge: Polity Press.

Bourdieu, P. (1996) *Distinction: A Social Critique of the Judgement of Taste.* London: Routledge.

Bushnaq, I. (1986) *Arab Folktales.* Harmondsworth: Penguin.

Caracciolo, P. (1988) *The Arabian Nights in English Literature: Studies in the Reception of the Thousand and One Nights in British Culture.* New York: St Martin's Press.

Carbonell, O. (1996) The exotic space of cultural translation. In R. Álvarez and Vidal, C. (eds) *Translation, Power, Subversion* (pp. 79–98). Clevedon: Multilingual Matters.

Carbonell, O. (1997) *Traducir al Otro.* Cuenca: Universidad de Castilla-La Mancha.

Carbonell, O. (2001) Identity in translation. *Proceedings of the 1st Congress of Translation in Salamanca*, November 2000.

Carbonell, O. (2002) A cor què vols: sociolingüística de la traducció exotica. In P. Orero *et al.* (eds) *Volum homenatge a Dolors Cinca.* Barcelona: Universitat Autònoma de Barcelona.

Casagrande, J. (1954) The ends of translation. *International Journal of American Linguistics* 20, 335–40.

Chafe, W. (1982) Integration and involvement in speaking, writing, and oral literature. In D. Tannen (ed.) *Spoken and Written Language: Exploring Orality and Literacy* (pp. 35–53). Norwood, NJ: Ablex.

Chafe, W. and Tannen, D. (1987) The relation between written and spoken language. *Annual Review of Anthropology* 16: 383–407.

Chomsky, N.A. (1957) *Syntactic Structure.* The Hague: Mouton.

Clark, P. (1997) Contemporary Arabic literature in English. Why is so little translated? Do Arabs prefer it this way? *The Linguist* 36(4), 108–110.

Daif, al-, R. (1995) *Aziizi al-sayyid Kawabata*. al-Zalqa: Mukhtaraat. Translations: *Dear Mister Kawabata*, London, 1999; *Cher Monsieur Kawabata*, Arles, 1998; *Lieber Herr Kawabata*, Basel, 1998; *Estimado señor Kawabata*, Guadarrama, 1998; *Mio Caro Kawabata*, Rome, 1998; *Kochany Panie Kawabato*, Warsaw, 1998; *Kere herr Kawabata*, Stockholm, 1999.

Dallal, J.A. (1998, 24 April) The perils of occidentalism. *The Times Literary Supplement*, 8- 9.

Darwish, M. (1985) *Dhakira li nisyaan*. Translations: *Herinnering om te vergeten*, Amsterdam, 1996; *Una memoria per l'oblio*, Rome, 1997; *Memoria para el olvido*, Guadarrama, 1997.

Dijk, van. T.A. and Kintsch, W. (1983) *Strategies of Discourse Comprehension*. London: Academic Press.

Déjeux, J. (1982) *Situation de la littérature maghrébine de langue française*. Algiers: OPU.

Domb, R. (1982) *The Arab in Hebrew Prose 1911–1948*. London.

Dundes, A. (1980) Texture, text, and context. In *Interpreting Folklore*. Bloomington: Indiana University Press.

Eagleton, T. (1991) *Ideology. An Introduction*. London: Verso.

Eco, U. (1981) *Lector in fabula. La cooperación interpretativa en el texto narrativo*. Barcelona: Lumen.

Eisenstadt, S.N. (1954) *The Absorption of Immigrants*. London: Routledge and Kegan Paul.

El-Shamy, H. (1995) *Folk Traditions of the Arab World: A Guide to Motif Classification*. 2 Vols. Bloomington: Indiana University Press.

Enderwitz, S. (1998a) Notions of the self in Palestinian autobiographies. In *Beyrouth Zokak el-Blat(t)* 14.

Enderwitz, S. (1998b) From curriculum vitae to self-narration: Fiction in Arabic autobiography. In S. Leder (ed.) *Story-telling in the Framework of Non-fictional Arabic Literature*. Weisbaden: Harrassowitz Verlag.

Eshel, R. (1991) *Dancing with the Dream, the Advent of Artistic Dance in Palestine 1920– 1964*. Tel Aviv: Sifriyat Poalim Publishing House (in Hebrew).

Even-Zohar, I. (1990) *Polysystem Studies [= Poetics Today 11:1]*.

Faiq, S. (2000) Arabic translation: A glorious past but a meek present. In M.G. Rose (ed.) *Translation Perspectives XI: Beyond the Western Tradition* (pp. 83–98). Binghamton: State University of New York at Binghamton.

Faiq, S. (2001) Subverted representation in La Nuit Sacrée and its Arabic Translation. *International Journal of Francophone Studies (IJFS)* 4:1 (pp. 42–54).

Faiq, S. (2003) Your culture, my language: Representation and the master discourse of translation. In M. Williams (ed.) *Interaction Entre Culture et Traduction*. Tangier: ESRFT.

Farahidi, al-, Kh. (1980–1985) *Kitaab al-'ayn* (8 volumes). Makhzumi and Samirra'i (eds). Baghdad: Dar ar-Rashid.

Friedlander, Y. (1989) Metamorphoses and variations of the character of the alien in modern Hebrew literature. *Bulletin of the Israeli Academic Center in Cairo* 12, 41–4.

Gentzler, E. (1993) *Contemporary Translation Theories*. London: Routledge.

Ghanaim, M.H. (ed.) (1984–88) *Liqaa* 4, 5, 12. Kraf Saba: Beit Berl.

Guillaume, A. (1990) *Islam*. London: Penguin Books.

Guth, S. (1998) Why novels – not autobiographies? An essay in the analysis of a historical development. In R. Ostle, Ed de Moor and S. Wild (eds) *Writing the Self. Autobiographical Writing in Modern Arabic Literature* (pp. 139–47). London: Saqi Books.

Gutt, E-A (1991) *Translation and Relevance: Cognition and Context.* Cambridge: Basil Blackwell.

Halliday, M.A.K. and Hassan, R. (1976) *Cohesion in English.* London: Longman.

Hatim, B. (1997) *Communication Across Cultures.* Exeter: University of Exeter Press.

Hatim, B. and Mason, I. (1990) *Discourse and the Translator.* London: Longman.

Henkin, R. (1996) Negev Bedouin vs. Sedentary Palestinian narrative styles. *Israel Oriental Studies,* Vol. 16 (169–91).

Hilali, al-, M.T. and Khan, M.M. (1983) *Translation of the Meanings of the Noble Qur'an in the English Language.* Madina, Saudi Arabia: King Fahd Complex.

Holquist, M. (1994) *Dialogism: Bakhtin and his World.* London: Routledge.

Hymes, D. (1981) *In Vain I Tried to Tell You: Essays in Native American Ethnopoetics.* Philadelphia: University of Pennsylvania Press.

Irving, T.B. (1985) *The Qur'an: The First American Translation.* Brattleboro: Amana Books.

Irwin, R. (1994) *The Arabian Nights: A Companion.* New York: The Penguin Press.

Ithima, M.A. (1972) *Dirasa li-uslub al-Qur'an al-Karim.* 1–11 volumes. Cairo: Dar al-Hadith.

Itkonen, E. (1991) *Universal History of Linguistics: India, China, Arabia, Europe.* Amsterdam: John Benjamins.

Jabra, I. J. (1986) *al-Bi'r al-'ula.* London: Riad El-Rayyes Translations: *Der erste Brunnen,* Basel, 1997; *I Pozzi de Betlemme,* Rome, 1997; *El primer pozo,* Guadarrama, 1997; *Els pous de Betlem,* Barcelona, 1999.

Jacquemond, R. (1992) Translation and cultural hegemony: The case of French-Arabic translation. In L. Venuti (ed.) *Rethinking Translation* (pp. 139–58). London and New York: Routledge;

Jacquemond, R. (1993) Traductions croisées Egypte-France: Stratégies de traduction et échange culturel inégal. *Egypte/Monde Arabe* 15–16, 283–95.

Jad, A. (1983) *Form and Technique in the Egyptian Novel 1912–1971.* London: Itaca.

Janabi, al-, A. (1995) *Tarbiyat al-Janabi.* Translations: *Vertikale Horizonte – Von Bagdad nach Paris,* Basel 1997; *Horizon Vertical,* Arles, 1998; *L'horitz vertical,* Barcelona, 1998.

Jenkins, R. (1992) *Pierre Bourdieu.* London: Routledge.

Kabbani, R. (1989) *Europe's Myths of Orient.* London: Pandora.

Karim, H.K. (1997) The historical resilience of primary stereotypes: Core images of the Muslim other. In S.H. Riggins (ed.) *The Language and Politics of Exclusion* (pp. 153–82). London: Sage.

Kathir, Ibn (1993) *Tafsir al-Qur'an and al-Athim.* Vol. 4. Beirut: Mu'ssasat al-Kutub al-Thaqafiyyah.

Kievet, R. (1990) Four moot points in literary translation. In B. Westerweel and T. D'haen (eds) *Something Understood: Studies in Anglo-Dutch Literary Translation* (pp. 319–29). Amsterdam: Rodopi.

Kilpatrick, H. (1974) *The Modern Arabic Novel: A Study in Social Criticism.* London: Itaca.

Lambert, J. (1989) La traduction. In M. Angenot, J. Bessière, D. Fokkema and E. Kushner (eds) *Théorie littéraire* (pp. 151–9). Paris: PUF.

Lane, E.W. (1863) *An Arabic-English Lexicon* (8 parts). London: William and Norgate.

Laor, Y. (1995) *Narratives with No Natives. Essays on Israeli Literature.* Tel Aviv: Hakibbutz HaMeuchad Publishing House (in Hebrew).

Larrimendi, M. de and Parilla, G. (eds) (1997) *Pensiamento y Circulación de las Ideas en el Mediterráneo: el Papel de la Traducción*. Cuanca: Ediciones de la Universidad de Castilla-La Mancha.

Layoun, M. (1995) Translation, cultural transgression and tribute, and leaden feet. In A. Dingwaney and C. Maier (eds) *Between Languages and Cultures* (pp. 267–89). Pittsburgh: University of Pittsburgh Press.

Leeuwen, R. van (1981) Literature and politics in Egypt. *MERA-Essays* 1.

Leeuwen, R. van (1998a) Two Egyptians at the World Exhibition in Paris. In R. Ostle, Ed de Moor and W. Stefan (eds) *Writing the Self: Autobiographical Writing in Modern Arabic Literature*. London: Saqi Books.

Leeuwen, R. van (1998b) Autobiography, travelogue and identity. In R. Ostle, Ed de Moor and S. Wild (eds) *Writing the Self. Autobiographical Writing in Modern Arabic Literature* (pp. 27–9). London: Saqi Books.

Leeuwen, R. van (2000a) Visions of power in *Awlad haratina* of Naguib Mahfouz. In M. de Larrimendi and L. Cacada (eds) *La Traducción de Literatura Arabe Contemporanea: Antes y Después de Naguib Mahfuz*. Cuenca: Ediciones de la Universidad de Castilla-La Mancha.

Leeuwen, R. van (2000b) Literary journalism and the field of literature: the case of *Akhbar al-adab*. *Quaderni di Studi Arabi*, vol. 18.

Lefevere, A. (1990) Translation: Its genealogy in the West. In S. Bassnett and A. Lefevere (eds.) *Translation, History and Culture* (pp. 14–28). London: Cassell.

Lefevere, A. (1996) Translation: Who is doing what for / against whom and why? In M.G. Rose (ed.) *Translation Horizons Beyond the Boundaries of Translation Spectrum [Translation Perspectives IX]* (pp. 45–58). Binghamton: State University of New York at Binghamton.

Longacre, R.E. (1983) *The Grammar of Discourse*. London: Plenum Press.

Lorscher, W. (1991) *Translation Performance, Translation Process and Translation Strategies: A Psycholinguistic Investigation*. Tubingen: Gunter Narr Verlag.

Lüthi, M. (1976) *Once Upon a Time: On the Nature of Fairy Tales*. Trans. Lee Chadeayne and Paul Gottwald. Bloomington: Indiana University Press.

Lüthi, M. (1982) *The European Folktale: Form and Nature*. Trans. John D. Niles. Philadelphia: Institute for the Study of Human Issues.

Lüthi, M. (1984) *The Fairytale as Art Form and Portrait of Man*. Trans. Jon Erickson. Bloomington: Indiana University Press.

MacKenzie, J.M. (1995) *Orientalism: History, Theory and the Arts*. Manchester: Manchester University Press

Makdisi, S. (1995) Post-colonial literature in a neo-colonial world: modern Arabic culture and the end of modernity. *Boundary* 2, 85–115.

Mamdouh, A. (1986) *Habbat naftalin*. Translations: *Mottenballen*, Rijswijk, 1998; *Mottenkugeln*, Basel, 1998; *Naftalina*, Rome, 1999.

Mason, I. (1995) Discourse, ideology, and translation. In R. de Beaugrande *et al.* (eds) *Language, Discourse and Translation in the West and Middle East* (pp. 23–34). Amsterdam: John Benjamins,.

Mazini, al-, I. (1971) *Qissat Hayah*. Cairo: Dar ash-sha'b.

Mehrez, S. (1992) Translation and the postcolonial experience: The francophone North-African texts. In L. Venuti (ed) *Rethinking Translation* (pp. 120–38). London and New York: Routledge.

Mehrez, S. (1994) *Egyptian Writers Between History and Fiction*: Cairo: American University of Cairo.

Michael, S. (1993) Hunting the gazelle. In S. Somekh (ed.) *Translation as a Challenge, Papers on Translation of Arabic Literature into Hebrew* (pp. 7–10). Tel Aviv: Tel Aviv University and the Institute for Arabic Studies, Givat Haviva (in Hebrew).

Mira, J.F. (1999, September) La piràmide de Bent. *El Temps Setmnari d'informació general*, 114.

Morson, G.S. and Caryl, E. (1990) *Mikhail Bakhtin: Creation of a Prosaics*. Stanford: Stanford University Press.

Mounif, A.R. (1994) *Sirat madina*, Amman. Translations: *Story of a City*, London, 1996; *Une ville dans la mémoire*, Arles, 1996; *Verhaal van een stad*, Breda 1996, *Storia di una città*, Rome, 1996, *Geschichte einer Stadt*, Basel 1996; *Memoiria de una ciudad*, Guadarrama, 1996, *Història d'una ciutat*, Barcelona, 1996.

Muhawi, I. (1996) Language, ethnicity, and national identity in the Tunisian ethnic joke. In Y. Suleiman (ed.) *Language and Identity in the Middle East and North Africa* (pp. 39–59). Richmond, Surrey: Curzon Press.

Muhawi, I. (2002) Performance and translation in the Arabic metalinguistic joke. *The Translator* 6 (2), 341–66 (Special Issue on Humour).

Muhawi, I. and Kanaana, S. (1989) *Speak, Bird, Speak Again: Palestinian Arab Folktales*. Berkeley and Los Angeles: University of California Press.

Musa, abu-, M.M. (1988) *Al-Balagha al-Qur'aniyya fi Tafsir al-Zamakhshari wa Atharuha fi al-Dirasat al-Balaghiyya*. Cairo: Maktabat Wahba.

Musaad-Basta, R. (1994) *BayDat n-na'ama*. London: Riad El-Rayyes. Translations: *El huevo del avestruz*, Guadarrama, 1997; *L'Oeuf de l'autruche*, Arles, 1997; *Luovo di struzzo*, Rome, 1998.

Nir, Y. (1985) *The Bible and the Image, the History of Photography in the Holy Land 1839–1899*. Philadelphia: University of Pennsylvania Press.

Niranjana, T. (1992) *Siting Translation: History, Poststructuralism and the Colonial Context*. Berkeley: University of California Press.

Olney, J. (1973) *Tell Me Africa: An Approach to African Literature*. Princeton: Princeton University Press.

Olney, J. (1980) Autobiography and the cultural moment: A thematic, historical and bibliographical introduction. In J. Olney (ed.) *Autobiography: Essays Theoretical and Critical* (pp. 3–27). Princeton: Princeton University Press.

Ong, W.J. (1982) *Orality and Literacy: The Technologizing of the Word*. London and New York: Routledge.

Ostle, R. (1998) Introduction. In R. Ostle, Ed de Moor and S. Wild (eds) *Writing the Self. Autobiographical Writing in Modern Arabic Literature* (pp. 18–23). London: Saqi Books.

Palva, H. (1977) The descriptive imperative of narrative style in spoken Arabic. *Folia Orientalia* XVIII, 5–26.

Palva, H. (1984) Further notes on the descriptive imperative of narrative style in Arabic. *Studia Orientalia* 55, 3–15.

Palva, H. (1992) *Artistic Colloquial Arabic: Traditional Narratives and Poems from al-Balqa' (Jordan)*. Studia Orientalia, 69.

Peña, S. (1999) El traductor en su jaula: hacia una pauta de análisis de traducciones. In E. Morillas and J.P. Arias (eds) *El Papel del Traductor* (19–57). Salamanca: Colegio de España.

Perry, M. (1986) The Israeli-Palestinian conflict as a metaphor in recent Israeli fiction. *Poetics Today* 7 (4), 603–19.

Pickthall, M. (1969) *The Meaning of the Glorious Qur'an: An Explanatory Translation*. London: George Allen and Unwin.

Pipes, D. (1990) *The Rushdie Affair: The Novel, the Ayatollah, and the West*. New York: Birch Lane Press.

Potter, J. (1996) *Representing Reality. Discourse, Rhetoric and Social Construction*. London, Thousand Oaks and New Delhi: Sage Publications. Spanish translation by G. Sánchez Barberán, *La Representación de la Realidad*. Barcelona: Paidós (1998).

Qattan, al-, M. (1990) *Mabahith fi Ulum al-Qur'an*. Cairo: Maktabat Wahbah.

Qurtubi, al-, A.M. (1997) *al-Jami' Liahkam al-Qur'an*. 1–20 Volumes. Beirut: Dar al-Kitab al Arabi.

Qutb, S. (1990) *Milestones*. Indianapolis: American Trust Publications.

Qutb, S. (1981) *Ma'aalim fi T-Tariiq*. Cairo: Dar al-Shuruq.

Rabassa, G. (1996) Words cannot express . . . the translation of cultures. In M.G. Rose (ed.) *Translation Horizons Beyond the Boundaries of Translation Spectrum [Translation Perspectives IX]* (pp. 183–94). Binghamton: State University of New York at Binghamton.

Ramraus-Rauch, G. (1989) *The Arab in Israeli Literature*. Indiana: Indiana University Press.

Rooke, T. (1997) *In My Childhood: A Study of Arabic Autobiography*. Stockholm: Almqvist and Wiksell International.

Ross, B. (1996) Zum autobiographischen bei Salim Barakat. *Asiatische Studien*, L2, 407- 29.

Rushdie, S. (1991) *Imaginary Homelands: Essays and Criticism 1981–1991*. London: Viking.

Ruthven, M. (1990) *A Satanic Affair: Salman Rushdie and the Rage of Islam*. London: Chatto and Windus.

Said, E. (1979) *Orientalism*. New York: Vintage Books.

Said, E. (1993) *Culture and Imperialism*. London: Chatto and Windus.

Said, E. (1995) Embargoed literature. In A. Dingwaney and C. Maier (eds) *Between Languages and Cultures* (pp. 97–102). Pittsburgh: University of Pittsburgh Press.

Said, E. (1997) *Covering Islam*. London: Vintage. (First published by Routledge and Kegan Paul, 1981).

Sapir, E. (1921) *Language: An Introduction to the Study of Speech*. New York: Harcourt, Brace and World.

Sara, S.I. (1991) Al-Khaliil the first Arab phonologist. *International Journal of Arabic and Islamic Linguistics* 7, 1–57.

Sara, S.I. (1993) The beginning of phonological terminology in Arabic. In K. Dévényi *et al.* (eds) *Proceedings of the Colloqium on Arabic Lexicology and Lexicography* (pp. 181–94). Budapest: Eötvös Lorand University.

Sara, S.I. (1996) Umlauting in Sibawaih. In K.R. Jankawsky (ed.) *Multiple Perspectives on the Historical Dimensions of Language* (pp. 255–67). Munster: Nodus Publications.

Sayyid, B. (1997) *A Fundamental Fear*. London: Zed Books.

Schnitzer, M. (1994) *Israeli Cinema – All the Facts, All the Plots, All the Directors and Some Reviews*. Tel Aviv: Rinneret Publishing House (in Hebrew).

Schwarz, W. (1955) *Principles and Problems of Biblical Translation*. London: Cambridge University Press.

Seitel, P. (1980) *See So That We May See: Performances and Interpretations of Traditional Tales from Tanzania*. Bloomington: Indiana University Press.

Shakir, M. (1926) On the translation of the Koran into foreign languages. *Muslim World* 16, 161–5.

Shammas, A. (ed.) (1975) *Bi Saut Muzdawij, an Anthology of Texts by Jewish and Arab Writers by their own Choice.* Haifa: Bayt al-Karma.

Shammas, A. (ed.) (1976) *Bi Saut Muzdawij, an Anthology of Texts by Jewish and Arab Writers by their own Choice.* Haifa: Bayt al-Karma.

Shammas, A. (1985) On right and left in translation. *Iton* 77, 64–65 (in Hebrew).

Sharaf, A. (1992) *Adab al-Sira al-Dhatiyya.* Beirut: Maktabat Lubnaan.

Sibawaih, A.B. (1898) *al-Kitaab* (2 vols). Bulaq: al-MaTba'ah al-Kubraa al-'amiriyyah.

Sibawaih, A.B. (1881/1970) *Le Livre de Sibwaih* (2 vols), Hartwig Derenbourg (ed.). Hildesheim: Georg Olms Verlag.

Somekh, S. (1973) *The Changing Rhythm, A Study of Najib Mahfuz's Novels.* Leiden: E.J. Brill.

Sprinker. M. (ed.) (1992) *Edward Said: A Critical Reader.* Oxford: Blackwell.

Stagh, M. (1999) The translation of Arabic literature into Swedish. In The translation of contemporary Arabic literature in Europe, *Cuadernos* 2 (pp. 41–6). Escuela de traductores de Toledo.

Tannen, D. (1989) *Talking Voices: Repetition, Dialogue, and Imagery in Conversational Discourse.* Cambridge: Cambridge University Press.

Tedlock, D. (1983) *The Spoken Word and the Work of Interpretation.* Philadelphia: University of California Press.

Thomas, S. (1998) Translating as intercultural conflict. In S. Hunston (ed.) *Language at Work* [British Studies in Applied Linguistics 13] (pp. 98–108). Clevedon: Multilingual Matters.

Tomiche, N. (1978) *La Littérature Arabe Traduite. Mythes et Réalités.* Paris: Geuthner.

Toury, G. (1980) *In Search of a Theory of Translation.* Tel-Aviv: The Porter Institute for Poetics and Semiotics.

Toury, G. (1995) *Descriptive Translation Studies – and Beyond.* Amsterdam and Philadelphia: John Benjamins.

Troupeau, G. (1976) *Lexique-Index du Kitab de Sibawayhi.* Paris: Editions Klincksiek.

Turner, B.S. (1994) *Orientalism, Postmodernism and Globalism.* London: Routledge.

Turner, C. (1997) *The Qur'an: A New Interpretation.* Surrey: Curzon Press.

Urian, D. (1996) *The Arab in Israeli Theatre.* Or: Am Publishing House (in Hebrew).

Venuti, L. (1994) Translation and the formation of cultural identities. *Current Issues in Language and Society* 1(3), 201–19.

Venuti, L. (1995) *The Translator's Invisibility: A History of Translation.* London and New York: Routledge.

Venuti, L. (1996) Translation as social practice: Or, the violence of translation. In M.G. Rose (ed.) *Translation Horizons Beyond the Boundaries of Translation Spectrum* [*Translation Perspectives IX*] (pp. 195–214). Binghamton: State University of New York at Binghamton.

Venuti, L. (1998) *The Scandals of Translation. Towards an Ethics of Difference.* London and New York: Routledge.

Versteegh, C. (1977) *Greek Elements in Arabic Linguistic Thinking.* Leiden: Brill.

Yahudah, A. S. (1896) Arab heroes and noblemen. In *Luah Eretz Yisrael.* Jerusalem: Lunz Publishing House (in Hebrew).

Young, R. (1990) *White Mythologies: Writing History and the West.* London: Routledge.

Zalmona, Y. and Manor-Friedman, T. (1998) To the East: Orientalism in the arts in Israel. *Catalogue* 404. Jerusalem: The Israel Museum (in Hebrew).

Zamakhshari, al-, Q. (1995) *al-Kashshaf.* (1–4 Volumes). Beirut: Dar al-Kutub al-Ilmiyyah.
Zayn, al-, S.A. (1985). *al-'I'rab fi al-Qur'an al-Karim.* Beirut: Dar al-Kitab al-Lubnani.
Zayyat, L. (1992) *Hamlat taftish: awraq shakhsiyya,* Cairo: Kitab al-hilal. Translations: *The Search,* London, 1996; *Perquisition!,* Arles, 1996, *Het Onderzoek,* Breda, 1996, *Carte private di una femminista,* Rome, 1996; *Durchsuchungen,* Basel, 1996; *Notas personales,* Guadarrama, 1999.
Ziyadeh, Kh. (1994) *Yawm al-jum'a, yawm al-aHad,* Beirut: Dar al-nahaar. Translations: *Vendredi, Dimanche,* Arles, 1996; *Viernes y Domingos,* Guadarrama, 1996, *Venerdi, Domenica,* Rome, 1996, *Freitag, Sontag,* Basel, 1996.
Zlateva, P. (1990) Translation: Text and pre-text. Adequacy and Acceptability in cross-cultural communication. In S. Bassnett and A. Lefevere (eds) *Translation, History, Culture* (pp. 29–37). London: Cassell.

Index

Authors

Subjects